Quotable
Quotes
for
Quoters

Quotable Quotes for Quoters

by

Aubrey Malone

CONTENTS

FOREWORD

Over the past number of years I've been jotting down sayings by the famous – and indeed unfamous – if they amused me or otherwise engaged my attention. This started as a hobby but as the file grew I eventually realised I had enough for a book – the one you're now holding in front of you. As well as entertaining and/or enlightening you, I hope the quotes will be of help to those of you looking for little nuggets of wit and wisdom to embellish a speech you might be endeavouring to prepare.

That's why I've divided the quotations up into topics, to help speech-makers find their way round quickly and easily.

So whether you're simply dipping into these pages to pass a few hours or are engaged in a more desperate search for some pithy words to spice that all-important wedding speech, I'm sure you'll find something here to make you (and your audience) chuckle.

ADVICE

It is a good thing for an uneducated man to read
books of quotations. *Winston Churchill*

To try and find out the reason for everything is very
dangerous and leads to nothing but disappointment.
Queen Victoria

The only thing to do with good advice is to pass it on.
It is never of any use to oneself. *Oscar Wilde*

If you don't raise your eyes, you'll think you're at the
highest point. *Antonio Porchia*

Everybody should wear contact lenses, whether they
need them or not. *Morrissey*

It is only shallow people who do not judge by
appearances. *Oscar Wilde*

Never let your schooling interfere with your education.
Leonard Levinson

Talk to a man about himself and he will listen for hours.
Benjamin Disraeli

We should all learn to take things easily – other
people's things. *Harry Graham*

Santa Claus has the right idea: visit people once a year.
Victor Borge

The speeches to be wary of are those that begin, 'I'm just going to say a few words'.
Frank Muir

The only way to be absolutely safe is never to try anything for the first time.
Magnus Pyke

If you're giving your plants food, stop. If you're not feeding them, start immediately. This is based on the theory that whatever you're doing, it is bound to be wrong.
Miles Kington

There's just one rule about boxing: never bet on the white guy.
Lennox Lewis

Before criticising your wife's faults, pause to consider they might have prevented her marrying someone better than you.
Hal Roach

Don't tell your friends their faults. After they cure them, they'll never forgive you.
Logan Pearsall Smith

Never buy a portable TV set in the street from a man who's out of breath.
Arnold Glasgow

On the keyboard of life, always keep one finger on the Escape key.
Larry Dodgson

Here's a useful shopping tip: you can get a pair of shoes for £1 at bowling alleys.
Al Clethen

Don't worry about the world ending today – it's
already tomorrow in Australia.   *Steven Wright*

If you're dying in a lift, make sure you press the Up
button before you go.   *Jackie Mason*

Take things as you find them – but make sure no one
sees you.   *Leonard Levinson*

People who live in chateaux
Should never throw tomateaux.   *J B Morton*

In painting a ceiling a good rule of thumb is that there
should be at least as much paint on the ceiling as on
your hair.   *P J O'Rourke*

Never pick a fight with an ugly person. They've got
nothing to lose.   *Robbie Williams*

The one certain way for a woman to hold a man is to
leave him for religion.   *Muriel Spark*

When a man steals your wife, there is no better
revenge than to let him keep her.   *Sacha Guitry*

To jaw-jaw is always better than to war-war.
          Winston Churchill

The only way to get rid of cockroaches is to tell them
you want a long-term relationship.   *Jasmine Birtles*

Start by saying no to requests. Then if you have to go to yes, okay. But if you start with yes, you can't go to no.

Mildred Perlman

Never trust a man with short legs. Brains too near their bottoms.

Noel Coward

Don't compare yourself – you're all you've got.

Janis Joplin

If you want to know who your friends are, get yourself a jail sentence.

Charles Bukowski

Don't bite your nails – look what happened to Venus de Milo.

Sammy Davis Jnr

Speak when you're angry and you will make the best speech you will ever regret.

Ambrose Bierce

It is not economical to go to bed early to save the candles if the result is twins.

Chinese proverb

Never approach a friend's girlfriend or wife with mischief as your goal – unless she's really attractive.

Bruce Friedman

Please write music like Wagner, only louder.

Samuel Goldwyn to a movie music composer

If you only ever read one book in your life, I strongly recommend . . . you keep your mouth shut.

Simon Munnery

In baiting a mousetrap with cheese, always leave room for the mouse. **Saki**

Never trust a man who, when he's alone in a room with a tea cosy, doesn't try it on. **Billy Connolly**

Never invest your money in anything that eats. **Billy Rose**

Start thinking positively. You'll notice a difference. Instead of 'I think I'm a loser', try 'I definitely am a loser'. Stop being wishy-washy about things. How much more of a loser can you be if you don't even know you're one? **Ellen Degeneres**

The best way to get husbands to do something is to suggest that they are too old to do it. **Shirley MacLaine**

To lead the people, walk behind them. **Lao Tsu**

Vote for the man who promises least. He'll be the least disappointing. **Jacques Barzun**

Never eat lettuce in Mexico unless it's been sterilised by a blowtorch. **Benjamin Kean**

Always say no to drugs. It will drive the prices down. **Jim Davidson**

Always choose the oldest customs official. No chance of promotion. **W Somerset Maugham**

If you want to get rich from writing, write the sort of thing that's read by people who move their lips as they read.   *Don Marquis*

There are two ways to live your life. One is as though nothing is a miracle. The other is as though everything is a miracle.   *Albert Einstein*

If you want the world to beat a path to your door, just try to take a nap on a Saturday afternoon.   *George Brown*

If we are to abolish the death penalty, let the murderers take the first step.   *Alphonse Karr*

If you're given a choice between money and sex appeal, take the money. As you get older, the money will become your sex appeal.   *Katharine Hepburn*

Fuel is more effectively delivered coal-de-sack than a la cart.   *Graffiti*

If something pleasant happens to you, don't forget to tell it to your friends to make them feel bad.
Casimir Montrond

Turn on, tune in, drop out.   *Timothy Leary*

Get your facts first, and then you can distort them as much as you please.   *Mark Twain*

Always listen to the professionals . . . and then do the opposite of what they say.   *H L Mencken*

Never drink black coffee at lunch. It will keep you awake in the afternoon.
Jilly Cooper

Don't jump on a man unless he's down.
Finley Peter Dunne

Remember the poor. It costs nothing.
Josh Billings

Early to rise and early to bed, makes a man healthy, wealthy and dead.
James Thurber

Never trust anyone who wears a beard, a bow tie, two-toned shoes or sunglasses.
Michael Caine

If you're foolish enough to be contented, don't show it. Grumble with the rest.
Jerome K Jerome

If you send your dog to fetch the paper, make sure it knows which one to get, and don't give it too much money or it might not come back.
Mike Harding

Never lend books, for no one ever returns them. The only books I have in my library are ones that other folk have lent me.
Anatole France

Always suspect everybody.
Charles Dickens

Don't spend £2 to dry-clean a shirt. Donate it to the Salvation Army instead. They'll clean it for you and put it on a hanger. Then you can buy it back for 50p.
Jack Dee

It's not a good time to use lifts during fires. Fire
extinguishers are much more effective.   *P J O'Rourke*

If you haven't got any socks, you can't pull them up.
Jeffrey Bernard

Never go to a doctor whose office plants have died.
Erma Bombeck

Do not do unto others as you would they should do
unto you. Their tastes may not be the same.
George Bernard Shaw

After you've done a thing the same way for two years,
look it over carefully. After five years look at it with
suspicion . . . and after ten throw it away and start all
over again.   *Alfred Pearlman*

Never share a foxhole with anyone braver than you are.
H L Mencken

Persuade the decision-makers that the decision you
want is their idea.   *Michael Shea*

Don't make jokes at the European Parliament. You'll
find the Germans only get them ten minutes after the
Swedes.   *Glenys Kinnock*

If you want to scare your boyfriend next Halloween,
come dressed as what he fears most: commitment.
Peter Nelson

If you want to become a coroner, be prepared for a stiff examination.

John Crosbie

The best time to enjoy a European trip is about three weeks after unpacking.

George Ade

Do not fear when your enemies criticise you. Beware when they applaud.

Ralph Waldo Emerson

Avoid the Christmas rush – panic now.

Joe Joyce

Never believe anything until it's been officially denied.

Katharine Whitehorn

To be successful, keep looking tanned, live in an elegant building (even if you're in the cellar), be seen in smart restaurants (even if you nurse one drink), and if you borrow, borrow big.

Aristotle Onassis

Advice is seldom welcome, and those who want it the most always like it the least.

Lord Chesterfield

Advice after injury is like medicine after death.

Proverb

Join the army, see the world, meet interesting people – and kill them.

Pacifist badge

When you have nothing to say, say nothing.

Charles Colton

The most popular speaker is the one who sits down before he stands up.

J P Mahaffy

I don't go with feminism. My advice to women is to marry a rich guy with a bad heart, then creep up behind him and go 'Boo!'. *Joan Rivers*

Let's remind ourselves that last year's fresh idea is this year's cliché. *Austen Briggs*

When a man tells me he's going to put all his cards on the table, I always look up his sleeves. *Leslie Belisha*

You're either part of the solution or you're part of the problem. *Eldridge Cleaver*

Problems are only opportunities in workclothes. *Henry Kaiser*

There's no way to make people like change. You can only make them feel less threatened by it. *Frederick Hayes*

If you're planning for one year, plant rice. If you're planning for ten years, plant trees. If you're planning for 100 years, plant people. *Indian proverb*

Beware of the conversationalist who says, 'In other words'. He is merely starting afresh. *Robert Morley*

Before you criticise someone, you should walk a mile in their shoes. That way, when you criticise them, you are a mile away from them, and you have their shoes. *Frieda Norris*

We all know what happens to people who stay in the middle of the road. They get run over.   *Aneurin Bevan*

Don't argue with a woman in the kitchen. We know where everything is and you don't.   *Diane Amos*

There's no formula for success, but there's a formula for failure – trying to please everyone.   *Nicholas Ray*

If it moves, salute it. If it doesn't move, pick it up. If you can't pick it up, paint it.   *Paul Dickinson*

Never play cards with a man called Doc. Never eat at a place called Mom's. Never sleep with a woman whose troubles are worse than your own.   *Nelson Algren*

Marry an archaeologist – the older you get, the more interested he is in you.   *Agatha Christie*

They say hard work never killed anyone, but I figured, why take the chance?   *Ronald Reagan*

If in any doubt, file under H for 'Haven't A Clue'.
    Lily Tomlin

When you're skinning your customers, you should leave some skin on to grow so you can skin them again.
    Nikita Khrushchev

Be nice to people on the way up – because you'll meet them on the way down as well.   *Wilson Mizner*

You need someone to love while you're looking for someone to love.   *Shelagh Delaney*

Better murder an infant in its cradle than nurse an unacted desire.   *William Blake*

To avoid eye contact, kiss.   *Mason Cooley*

Never talk about money to people who have much more or less of it than you.   *Katharine Whitehorn*

When you seek advice from someone, it's certainly not because you want them to give it. You just want them to be there while you talk to yourself.   *Terry Pratchett*

Drive like hell – you'll get there.   *Road Safety slogan*

The surest way to a woman's heart is to aim kneeling.   *Douglas Jerrold*

Don't give a woman advice. One should never give a woman anything she can't wear in the evening.   *Oscar Wilde*

We must laugh before we are happy, for fear of dying without having laughed at all.   *Jean de La Bruyère*

Stop smoking – carry wet matches.   *Bob Monkhouse*

Don't throw cigarettes in the toilet bowl. It makes them all soggy.   *Graffiti*

If the grass is greener in the other fellow's garden, let him worry about mowing it. *Paddy Murray*

Don't be too hard on your relatives; it's not their fault either. *Jasper Carrott*

Don't put the cat out unless it's on fire. *Hal Roach*

Of all the 36 alternatives, running away is best. *Chinese proverb*

Don't look back. Something may be gaining on you. *Satchel Paige*

If you ever want a thing well done, get a couple of old broads to do it. *Bette Davis*

A friend of mine wrote a book called *How to Attract Men*. Her main advice is to be naked and have a bar by your bed. *John Waters*

Don't pay any attention to critics. Don't even ignore them. *Samuel Goldwyn*

If you're bored with your present enemies and want to make some new ones, tell two of your women friends that they look alike. *Mignon McLaughlin*

In any war movie, never share a foxhole with a character who carries a photo of his sweetheart. *Del Close*

Here's a tip to stop smoking: douse yourself in petrol every day.
                                                    Bill Bailey

Write something, even if it's only a suicide note.
                                                    Gore Vidal

Always be sincere even if you don't mean it.
                                                    Harry S Truman

When angry, count to four. When very angry, swear.
                                                    Mark Twain

Beware the fury of a patient man.   *John Dryden*

Never transmit a sexual disease in public.   *P J O'Rourke*

Don't wreck a sublime chocolate experience by feeling guilty. Chocolate isn't like pre-marital sex. It will not make you pregnant.   *Lara Brody*

Never trust the advice of a man in difficulties.   *Aesop*

Flattery is all right as long as you don't inhale.
                                                    Adlai Stevenson

Never go to a dentist with blood in his hair.
                                                    William Ruskin

If you're going to be able to look back on something and laugh about it, you may as well laugh about it now.
                                                    Marie Osmond

Be wiser than other people if you can, but don't tell them so.   *Philip Stanhope*

The stupid neither forgive nor forget. The naïve forgive and forget. The wise forgive but do not forget.

Thomas Szasz

The easiest way to find something you've lost is to buy another one. Then the original will turn up the next day.

Leonard Rossiter

Don't be humble. You're not that great.

Golda Meir

Never take anybody's advice.

George Bernard Shaw

AGE

The secret of eternal youth is to lie about your age.

Bob Hope

Growing old is like being increasingly penalised for a crime you haven't committed.

Anthony Powell

The years a woman subtracts from her age aren't lost: they're added onto other women's.

Diane de Poitiers

Retirement at 65 is ridiculous. When I was 65 I still had pimples.

George Burns

At the age of 20 we don't care what the world thinks of us. At the age of 30 we worry about what it thinks. At 40 we realise it isn't thinking about us at all.

Herbert Prochnow

One of the more depressing experiences of middle life
is trying on your old RAF jacket and finding that the
only part of it that still fits you is the tie.   *Denis Norden*

The only thing that can be said in favour of the future
is the fact that we haven't the foggiest what it holds for
us.   *Paul Lynch*

Life is just a symphony of snap, crackle and pop.
When you're young it's the cornflakes; as you get older
it's the joints.   *Bob Hope*

One of the hardest decisions in life is when to start
middle age.   *Joan Rivers*

Every man over forty is a scoundrel.
      George Bernard Shaw

We are all geniuses up to the age of ten.   *Aldous Huxley*

Retirement is the ugliest word in the language.
      Ernest Hemingway

Women never have young minds. They were born
three thousand years old.   *Shelagh Delaney*

There are so many ways of us dying, it's astonishing
any of us choose old age.   *Beryl Bainbridge*

It's just as well to be told you're too old at 40. Then
you're over it.   *Sara C Medina*

Professionally, I have no age. *Kathleen Turner*

Middle age is the time when a man is always thinking that in a week or two he will feel as good as ever.
Don Marquis

You grow up the day you have your first real laugh at yourself. *Ethel Barrymore*

There are some advantages to getting old. First off, you're too deaf to hear your doctor saying 'You're gonna die'. Secondly, you get into the cinema at half price. They know you'll go again because you won't remember having seen the film before. *Joan Rivers*

Let me put the record straight. I'm 46, and have been for some years past. *Erica Jong*

People ought to retire at forty when they feel over-used . . . and go back to work at sixty-five when they feel useless. *Carol Anne O'Marie*

Virility at 21 is considered lechery at 71.
Dr George Giarchi

Suicide is much more acceptable in Hollywood than growing old gracefully. *Julie Birchill*

I'm at the age where my back goes out more than I do.
Phyllis Diller

Being 90 means getting up in the middle of the night
as often as Kevin Costner, but not for the same reason.
Bob Hope

At 18 our convictions are hills from which we look; at
45 they are caves in which we hide.   *F Scott Fitzgerald*

The richer the relative, the easier it is to remember
their birthday.   *Laurence J Peter*

They told me I wouldn't make 25. Then it was 35,
then 45. These were my doctors speaking – they're all
dead now.   *George Best*

The tragedy of old age is not that one is old but that
one is young.   *Oscar Wilde*

To go on living after forty is unseemly, disgusting and
immoral.   *Fyodor Dostoevsky*

At 50, everyone has the face he deserves.   *George Orwell*

If you want to know how old a woman is, ask her
sister-in-law.   *Ed Howe*

When a man of forty falls in love with a girl of twenty,
it's not her youth he's seeking, but his own.
Leonore Coffee

If you want to know what you'll look like in ten years'
time, look in the mirror after you've run a marathon.
Jeff Scaff

When you've reached a certain age and think that a facelift or a trendy way of dressing will make you feel twenty years younger, remember – nothing can fool a flight of stairs. *Denis Norden*

The young man who has not wept is a savage, and the old man who will not laugh is a fool. *George Santayana*

Men lie about their salaries, women about their ages. *Rita Rudner*

When a man fell into his anecdotage it was a sign for him to retire from the world. *Benjamin Disraeli*

If I'd known I was going to live this long I'd have taken better care of myself. *George Burns*

By the time your life is finished, you'll have learned just about enough to begin it well. *Eleanor Marx*

Life begins at forty. But so does lumbago, bad eyesight, arthritis, and the habit of telling the same story three times to the same person. *Pam Brown*

Thirty is a nice age for a woman, especially if she happens to be forty. *Phyllis Diller*

When we speak of people of a 'certain' age, we usually mean an uncertain one. *Patricia Casey*

A woman should hang on to her youth, but not while he's driving. *Jack Benny*

The secret of longevity is to stay breathing.

Sophie Tucker

Wrinkles are hereditary. Parents get them from their children.

Doris Day

Age is a question of mind over matter. If you don't mind, it doesn't matter.

Dan Ingrams

Nowadays 21 is about over the threshold of middle age for young executives.

Spike Lee

It's better to waste one's youth than to do nothing with it at all.

Georges Courteline

Middle age is when your age starts to show around the middle.

Bob Hope

By the time a man is wise enough to watch his step, he's too old to go anywhere.

Earl Wilson

Youth tends to look ahead. Old age tends to look back. Middle age tends to look worried.

James Simpson

For certain people after fifty, litigation takes the place of sex.

Gore Vidal

With sixty staring me in the face, I have developed inflammation of the sentence structure and a definite hardening of the paragraphs.

James Thurber

Any man under thirty who is not a liberal has no heart, and any man over thirty who is not a conservative has no brains.   *Winston Churchill*

You have to be over thirty to enjoy Proust.   *Gore Vidal*

Youth is a wonderful thing. What a crime to waste it on children.   *George Bernard Shaw*

Except for an occasional heart attack I feel as well as I ever did.   *Robert Benchley*

It's not necessarily true that you'll live longer if you don't drink, smoke, or chase women – it just *feels* like it.   *Anon*

We were planning to count the candles on his birthday cake, but we were driven back by the heat.   *Stuart Turner*

You're still young if the morning after the night before still makes the night before worth the morning after.   *Bob Goddard*

The only people who really adore being young are the middle-aged.   *Pam Brown*

She was 102. She didn't have wrinkles, she had *pleats*.   *Dennis Wolfberg*

Middle age is when you're faced with two temptations and you choose the one that will get you home by 9 o'clock.   *Ronald Reagan*

From birth to age 18 a girl needs good parents; from 18 to 35 she needs good looks; from 35 to 50 she needs a good personality. From 50 on, she needs good cash.   *Sophie Tucker*

Oh to be 70 again.
         Georges Clemenceau on his 80ᵗʰ birthday, after spotting a pretty girl

He's so old that when he orders a three-minute egg, they ask for the money upfront.   *Milton Berle*

I don't let old age bother me. There are three signs of old age. Loss of memory – I forget the other two.
                    Red Skelton

She was so old that when she went to school, they didn't have history.   *Rodney Dangerfield*

The most distressing thing about old age is that the hangovers last longer.   *Richard Harris*

If beauty is a letter of introduction, wrinkles are a good resumé.   *Mary Ellen Pickham*

I've been around so long I knew Doris Day before she was a virgin.   *Groucho Marx*

When women pass thirty, they first forget their age. When forty, they forget that they ever remembered it.
                    Ninon de Lenclos

Oh, to be only half as wonderful as my child thought I was when he was small, and only half as stupid as my teenager now thinks I am.   *Rebecca Richards*

Forty is the age when you stop patting yourself on the back and begin under the chin.   *Anon*

You know you're getting older when you try to straighten out the wrinkles in your socks – and discover you're not wearing any.   *Leonard L Knott*

I've got to the age where I need my false teeth and my hearing aid before I can ask where I've left my glasses.   *Stuart Turner*

Middle age is when your classmates are so old and bald they don't recognise you.   *Bennett Cerf*

My doctor said I look like a million dollars – green and wrinkled.   *Red Skelton*

One of the good things about growing older is that you find you're more interesting than most of the people you meet.   *Lee Marvin*

There are four stages of man: infancy, childhood, adolescence . . . and obsolescence.   *Art Linkletter*

You know, by the time you reach my age, you've made plenty of mistakes if you've lived properly.   *Ronald Reagan at 81*

CLOTHING

I base most of my fashion taste on what doesn't itch.
Gilda Radner

I wear the sort of clothes I wear to save me the trouble
of deciding what sort of clothes to wear.
Katharine Hepburn

A love of fashion makes the economy go round.
Liz Tilberg

On the whole, barristers are more interested in their
briefs than a woman's.
Jilly Cooper

Never wear your best trousers when you go out to fight
for truth and freedom.
Henrik Ibsen

As a general rule it's advisable to have your business
dress say nothing at all about you other than that your
clothes fit.
Mark McCormack

Moscow is a city where, if Marilyn Monroe should
walk down the street with nothing on but shoes,
people would stare at her feet.
John Gunther

The surest way to be out of fashion tomorrow is to be
in the forefront of it today.
Derek Marlowe

You know you're out of shape if the end doesn't justify
the jeans.
Coco Chanel

One book is very like another, something to read and
be done with. It's not a thing that matters, like print
dresses or serviettes.   *H G Wells*

To give him his due, Louis XIV brought the technique
of dressing and undressing in public to a perfection it
never reached before or since.   *Will Cuppy*

Queen Victoria wasn't a fashion leader. Probably the
most notable garment she ever wore was the nightdress
in which she received, that early morning at
Kensington Palace, the news of her uncle's death – the
nightdress in which she became Queen.
                                   Alison Adburgham

You ought to get out of those wet clothes and into a
dry martini.   *Mae West*

A sheep in sheep's clothing.
                     Winston Churchill on Clement Attlee

The car has become an article of dress without which
we feel uncertain, unclad and incomplete in the urban
compound.   *Marshall McLuhan*

He used to dress off the peg, but then the neighbours
decided to take in their washing.   *Paul Ryan*

If it wasn't for her girdle, her hourglass figure would
have a five o'clock bulge.   *Henny Youngman*

The reason I hate underwear and socks is that if you send twenty pairs of shorts and twenty pairs of socks to the Laundromat, you always get only nineteen back.

Andy Warhol

Women who wear tight clothes cause an impairment in breathing. Mine.

Benny Hill

I love people to see me naked because I was ashamed of the clothes I wore when I was young – the never-changing faded blue dress of poverty.

Marilyn Monroe

Men like cars and women like clothes. Women only like cars because they take them to the clothes.

Rita Rudner

Women speak because they wish to speak, whereas a man speaks only when driven to speech by something outside himself – like, for instance, he can't find any clean socks.

Jean Kerr

If God had meant us to walk around naked, he would never have invented the wicker chair.

Erma Bombeck

A dress makes no sense unless it inspires men to want to take it off you.

Françoise Sagan

Joan Crawford is the only actress to read the whole script. The rest just read their own lines to find out what clothes they're going to wear.

Anita Loos

Marilyn Monroe made it to the top because her dresses didn't.
Anon

Her hat looks as if it had made a forced landing on her head.
Red Skelton

Princess Diana wore more clothes in one day than Gandhi did in his entire life.
Joan Rivers

Miss Welch tottered by, clad in a brown jersey dress that appeared to be on the inside of her skin.
Maureen Lipman on Raquel Welch

Women who dress to please men should know that they don't have to dress to please men.
Mae West

Girls wear less on the street today than their grandmothers did in bed.
Barbara Cartland

Happiness is the sublime moment when you get out of your corsets at night.
Joyce Grenfell

Every kitchen should be equipped with a dishwasher, preferably a cute one wearing her apron and nothing else.
P J O'Rourke

Don't judge Cher by her clothes. There isn't enough evidence.
Bob Hope

I know a nudist who plays strip poker. Every time he loses he has to put something on.
Steven Wright

As martyrs burn for Christ, so ladies freeze for fashion.
C H Spurgeon

Behind every successful man stands a woman with
nothing to wear. *Harold Griffin*

The modern stocking will go into a spontaneous ladder
if you merely wink at it. *Ian Fraser*

From the cradle to the coffin, underwear comes first.
Bertolt Brecht

Fashion is made to become unfashionable. *Coco Chanel*

I always make the worst dressed list. It's kinda nice
having something you can count on. *Madonna*

Don't ever wear artistic jewellery: it wrecks a woman's
reputation. *Colette*

If you wear a woman's skirt it will help you get up the
stares. *Peter Cagney*

I may wear mink, but I think blue jeans. *Brigitte Bardot*

A bridegroom's mother is supposed to wear beige and
keep her mouth shut. *Erma Bombeck*

If the shoe fits, ask for it in another colour. *Beryl Pfizer*

I think nudity in films is disgusting. But if I were 22
with a great body it would be artistic, tasteful and a
progressive religious experience. *Shelley Winters*

In my heyday in films the photographers put me in low-necked nightgowns and told me to bend down and pick up pails. They were not photographing the pails.
Jane Russell

All women's dresses are merely variations on the eternal struggle between the admitted desire to dress and the unadmitted desire to undress.
Lin Yutang

I hold that gentleman to be the best dressed whose dress no one observes.
Anthony Trollope

You look rather rash, my dear. Your colours don't quite match your face.
Daisy Ashford

A fashionable woman is always in love with herself.
La Rochefoucauld

Fashion goes in one era and out the other.
Graffiti

One of the few lessons I have learned in life is that there is invariably something odd about women who wear ankle socks.
Alan Bennett

Women should observe one basic rule in clothing: never wear anything that panics the cat.
P J O'Rourke

I like clothes on other people, but they seem to suffer sea-change when they get on me. They deteriorate with a very strange rapidity until one feels really sorry for them.
Joyce Grenfell

DRINK

Alcohol is a liquid effective for preserving anything –
except secrets.   *Henny Youngman*

Far better than sex is the pleasure of drinking at
someone else's expense.   *Graffiti*

A mixture of brandy and water spoils two things.
                                                   Charles Lamb

Alcoholism is the only disease that tells you you don't
have a problem.   *Melanie Griffith*

The disease of niceness cripples more lives than
alcoholism.   *Robin Chandler*

Prohibition makes you want to cry into your beer and
denies you the beer to cry into.   *Don Marquis*

An abstainer is the sort of man you wouldn't want to
drink with even if he did.   *George Jean Nathan*

The best opener for a conversation is a bottle opener.
                                          Kevin Goldstein-Jackson

Whiskey is the most popular of the cold cure remedies
that don't work.   *Jerry Vale*

How do you look when I'm sober?   *Ring Lardner*

One tequila, two tequila, three tequila, floor.   *Graffiti*

An alcoholic is someone you don't like who drinks as much as you do. *Dylan Thomas*

If a man says he has conquered whiskey, you can be sure it is the whiskey that is doing the talking. *John B Keane*

Alcohol is necessary for a man so that he can have a good opinion of himself, undisturbed by the facts. *Finley Peter Dunne*

Be wary of strong drink. It can make you shoot at tax collectors – and miss! *Des MacHale*

Alcohol postpones anxiety, then multiplies it. *Mason Cooley*

Absinthe makes the heart grow fainter. *Bob Monkhouse*

If alcohol can be called a crutch, Jack Daniels whiskey is a wheelchair. *Frank Sinatra*

God invented whiskey so the Irish wouldn't rule the world. *Maureen Potter*

Alcoholism isn't a spectator sport. Eventually the whole family gets to play. *Joyce Burditt*

First you take a drink, then the drink takes a drink, then the drink takes you. *F Scott Fitzgerald*

Whiskey is the drink that makes you see double and feel single. **Dean Martin**

What, when drunk, one sees in other women, one sees in Garbo sober. **Kenneth Tynan**

One drink is ample. Two is too many. A hundred isn't enough. **Proverb**

I ruined my health drinking to other people's. **Brendan Behan**

If drinking is interfering with your work, you're probably a heavy drinker. If work is interfering with your drinking, you're probably an alcoholic. **Dr Anthony Clare**

If drink is the answer, what's the question? **Peter O'Toole**

It's no use saying drink is all right in moderation. Shall we have arsenic in moderation or murder in moderation? Wine is the juice of the grape gone bad. **Lord Soper, British clergyman**

Liquor is not a necessity. It is a means of momentarily side-stepping necessity. **Clifton Fadiman**

I've taken more pledges than drink. **Brendan Behan**

Drunks are rarely amusing unless they know some good songs and lose a lot at poker. **Karyl Roosevelt**

He'll probably never write a good play again.
*George Bernard Shaw on Eugene O'Neill after he gave up
alcohol*

When I don't feel well I drink, and when I drink I
don't feel well.   *W C Fields*

He drinks only to forget – but the only thing he
forgets is when to stop.   *Anon*

Alcohol is the most powerful depressant in the central
nervous system available without a doctor's
prescription. If it were being introduced now, it should
be a controlled drug.
Dr John Navard, secretary of the British Medical Association

When I'm playing a drunk I play him as a man trying
to be sober instead of a sober man trying to be drunk.
Michael Caine

It smells like gangrene; it tastes like the wrath to come
– and when you absorb a deep swig of it, you have all
the sensations of having swallowed a lighted kerosene
lamp.   *Irvin S Cobb*

I once saw Michael Scott take alternate sips of Scotch
and Alka Seltzer, thereby acquiring and curing a
hangover simultaneously.   *Hugh Leonard*

Did you hear about the time a petrol bomb was
thrown at Alex Higgins? He drank it.   *Frank Carson*

My favourite drink? The next one. **George Best**

Drink is our enemy. But the Bible says love your
enemies. **W C Fields**

My wife told me it was a disgrace coming home half
drunk. 'I know,' I said, 'but I ran out of money'.
Bob Monkhouse

The only cure for a real hangover is death.
Robert Benchley

Pour him outta here. **Mae West on W C Fields**

I used to jog but the ice-cubes kept falling out of my
glass. **David Lee Roth**

The telephone is a good way to talk to people without
having to offer them a drink. **Fran Lebowitz**

I'm allergic to alcohol. I break out in handcuffs.
Robert Downey Jnr

A man came to see me this morning absolutely reeking
of Horlicks. **Thomas Beecham**

A man shouldn't fool with booze until he's fifty, and
then he's a damn fool if he doesn't. **William Faulkner**

I saw a notice which said 'Drink Canada Dry' – and
I've just started. **Brendan Behan**

There are more old drunkards in the world than old
doctors.

Benjamin Franklin

There is no hangover on earth like the single malt
hangover. It roars in the ears, burns in the stomach and
sizzles in the brain like a short circuit. Death is the
easy way out.

Ian Bell

A well-balanced person has a drink in each hand.

Billy Connolly

It's better to drink to forget than to forget to drink.

Jackie Gleason

Alcohol is a very necessary article. It enables Parliament
to do things at eleven at night that no sane person
would do at eleven in the morning.

George Bernard Shaw

Have I a drinking problem? Yes – there's never enough.

Denis Thatcher

I have made an important medical discovery. Alcohol,
taken in sufficient quantities, produces the effects of
intoxication.

Oscar Wilde

I always keep a supply of stimulant handy in case I see
a snake – which I also keep handy.

W C Fields

There is no such thing as a small whiskey.

Oliver St John Gogarty

Please do not ask for credit as a kick in the face often
offends.

Pub Notice

An alcoholic is an egomaniac with an inferiority complex.   *Eugene O'Neill*

In vino headachitas.   *Graffiti*

My make-up wasn't smeared. I wasn't dishevelled. I behaved politely and I never finished off a bottle, so how could I be an alcoholic?
Betty Ford, who was one, but rehabilitated herself and went on to give her name to the famous drying-out centres in the US

The only thing I envy about young people is their livers.   *Brendan Behan*

I joined Alcoholics Anonymous, but there was no way I could be anonymous.   *George Best*

I drink to forget, but I can't remember what.
Dean Martin

Beer doesn't make you fat. It makes you lean – against tables, railings, bars . . .   *Rodney Dangerfield*

I spent my drinking years hitting people I liked and singing with my arm around people I loathed.
Billy Connolly

When I played drunks on screen I had to stay sober because I didn't know how to play them when I was drunk.   *Richard Burton*

Drinking won't solve your problems, but it will give you a lot of interesting new ones.   *Dean Martin*

Thou shalt not covet thy neighbour's house unless they
have a well-stocked bar. *W C Fields*

You can't drink all day if you don't start in the
morning. *Les Dawson*

There are five stages of drunkenness: verbose, jocose,
lachrymose, bellicose, comatose. *Jeffrey Bernard*

There are two things that will be believed of any man
whatsoever and one of them is that he has taken to
drink. *Booth Tarkington*

Confucius him say: people who drown sorrows would
be better off teaching them how to swim. *Bob Hope*

I hate to advocate drugs, alcohol, violence or insanity
to anyone but they've always worked for me.
Hunter S Thompson

Work is the curse of the drinking classes. *Oscar Wilde*

You're never as think as you drunk you are.
Frank Skinner

Don't drink anything stronger than gin before breakfast.
W C Fields

There's absolutely nothing wrong with sobriety in
moderation. *John Ciardi*

Reality is an illusion generated by the temporary
absence of alcohol. *Graffiti*

One reason I don't drink is because I want to know
when I'm having a good time.   *Nancy Astor*

Drink doesn't give you any answers – it just stops you
asking the questions.   *Frank Sinatra*

An alcoholic can always find a reason if he's thirsty. If
he's happy, he takes a couple of shots to celebrate his
happiness. Sad, he needs them to drown his sorrow.
Low, to pick him up; excited, to calm him down. Sick,
for his health – and healthy it can't hurt him. A lush
just can't lose.   *James Cagney*

Did it ever occur to you that the bottom of a bottle of
whiskey is much too near to the top?   *Sean O'Faolain*

Only ninnies make booze the excuse for their wild
escapades.   *Peter O'Toole*

My greatest ambition is to find the cure for a hangover.
          Terry Keane

A diplomat's life is made up of two ingredients: alcohol
and protocol.   *Adlai Stevenson*

No alcoholic is more dedicated to his cause than an
Irish one. It's almost like a religion. No less than total
commitment will do or you're not accepted into the
club.   *Brendan Kennelly*

Alcohol, for the Irish, is the emigration of the soul.
          John Waters

A Dublin drayman once pleaded that he was unfit for work because he had been to a christening the day before and the baby was the only one there that took water.   **Sean Desmond**

Driving whilst drunk these days is almost as dangerous as walking while sober.   **Herbert Prochnow**

The problem with me is that I should be drinking stout, but I can afford spirits.   **Brendan Behan**

George Best has cannibalised his illness for so long, it's almost become like a second career to him.
                                                    Tommy Conlon

EDUCATION

I gained my education at Eton during the holidays.
                                                    Osbert Sitwell

Today nearly everyone can read, but only a few can think.   **Cardinal Ottaviani**

Yesterday I couldn't spell engineer, now I are one.
                                                    Nigel Rees

I learn the way the monkey learns, from watching its parents.   **Prince Charles**

She has set herself an extremely low standard, which she has failed to maintain.

School report on Jilly Cooper, who subsequently became a best-selling novelist

Children's low maths grades today are usually due to a weak battery in their pocket calculators.   *Les Dawson*

It's only when you get the bill that you realise Higher Education really *is*.   *Bob Monkhouse*

After the average public school, the remainder of one's life, however unpleasant, cannot fail to seem something of a holiday.   *Osbert Sitwell*

Someday a PhD candidate will write a thesis on the average life of an undented fender on a Sunday afternoon.   *Herbert Prochnow*

The boy will go far – and the sooner he goes, the better.   *School report on James Balaam*

Education is a state-controlled manufactory of echoes.   *Norman Douglas*

Many children are backward at school because the school is too dull for them.   *A S Neill*

When the student is ready, the teacher appears.   *Lulu*

Education makes a people easy to lead but difficult to drive, easy to govern but difficult to enslave.   *Lord Henry Brougham*

The clever men at Oxford
Know all that there is to be knowed
But they none of them know one half as much
As intelligent Mr Toad.   *Kenneth Grahame*

Having no education, I had to use my brain.
                                 Bill Shankly

I would never send my son away to school unless I
hated him.   *Robbie Coltrane*

To live for a time close to great minds is the best form
of education.   *John Buchan*

Experience teaches us that it doesn't.   *Norman MacCaig*

Lack of education is an extreme handicap when one is
being offensive.   *Josephine Tey*

Why can't people learn to speak the truth? I have, I
think, taught two or perhaps three Indian colleagues to
do so. It will probably wreck their careers.
                                 J B S Haldene

Teaching drives a man to either drink, golf or insanity.
                                 John G Muir

Oxford University is a sanctuary in which exploded
systems and obsolete prejudices find shelter and
protection after they have been hunted out of every
corner of the world.   *Adam Smith*

The only saving grace of being at boarding school was freedom from my mother's cooking.   *Spike Milligan*

Anyone who has been to an English public school will always feel comparatively at home in prison.
Evelyn Waugh

When it came to education, my father wanted me to have all the benefits he never had . . . so he sent me to a girls' school.   *Eric Morecambe*

The difference between education and experience is this: education is when you read the fine print, and experience is when you don't.   *Pete Seeger*

Education is a method whereby one acquires a higher grade of prejudices.   *Laurence Peter*

Higher Education is a vacuum used to fill a vacuum.
J K Galbraith

Education is a mistake. Cluttering one's head with facts about anything other than oneself I hold to be a total waste of time.   *Quentin Crisp*

Illiteracy is bad, but not as bad as being able to read all the daily news.   *Auberon Waugh*

There's nobody as daft as an educated man once you get him off the subject he was educated in.   *Owen Kelly*

Schoolteachers are ludicrously underpaid as
childminders, and ludicrously overpaid as teachers.

John Osborne

Nothing that's worth knowing can be taught.

Oscar Wilde

I could never understand why a small child was
expected to write verses in Greek when he could
scarcely write his own name in English.   *Patrick Hastings*

An educated man should know something about
everything, and everything about something.

Dame Wedgwood

My degree was a kind of inoculation. I got just enough
education to make me immune to it for the rest of my
life.   *Alan Bennett*

No one who had any sense ever liked school.

Lord Boothby

The first problem for all of us, men and women, is not
to learn but to unlearn.   *Gloria Steinem*

The aim of education is to induce the largest amount
of neurosis the individual can bear without cracking.

W H Auden

Education enables you to earn more than the educator.

Benjamin Franklin

Academics like coming to conclusions, but not decisions.
Noel Annam

I generally spent my schooldays trying to find out how long it would take 6 men to build a wall if it took 3 of them a week. I seem to recall we spent as much time on the problem as the workmen spent on the wall.
Kenneth Tynan

It's only what you learn after you know it all that counts.
Harry Truman

ETHICS

None of the worst French novels from which careful parents try to protect their children can be as bad as what is daily laid upon the breakfast table of every educated family in England.
Queen Victoria on the reporting of divorce cases in newspapers in 1859

Truth is a rare and precious commodity so we should be sparing in its use.
C P Scott

It's always best to speak the truth – unless, of course, you're an exceptionally good liar.
Jerome K Jerome

As soon as one is unhappy, one becomes moral.
Marcel Proust

Don't put the blame where it belongs. Put it where it's easiest to disregard.
Joy Fielding

You can't learn too soon that the most useful thing about a principle is that it can always be sacrificed to expediency.   *W Somerset Maugham*

The fallacy of the liberal mind is to see good in everything. This has been of enormous assistance to the devil.   *Malcolm Muggeridge*

The greatest of faults . . . is to be conscious of none.
                    Thomas Carlyle

However harmless a thing is, if the law forbids it, most people will think it wrong.   *W Somerset Maugham*

It is possible to disagree with someone about the ethics of non-violence without wanting to kick his teeth in.
                    Christopher Hampton

Many are saved from sin by being so inept at it.
                    Mignon McLaughlin

If a man calls himself a realist, you can be sure he's about to do something he's ashamed of.   *Sydney Harris*

It is the function of vice to keep virtue within reasonable bounds.   *Samuel Butler*

To err is human, but it feels divine.   *Mae West*

The propriety of some persons seems to consist in having improper thoughts about their neighbours.
                    F H Bradley

I would rather be an opportunist and float than go to the bottom with my principles round my neck.

Stanley Baldwin

One should always play fairly when one has the winning cards.

Oscar Wilde

The best way to get over temptation is simply to yield to it.

Clementina Graham

No morals are better than bad ones.

Minna Antrim

Grub first, then ethics.

Bertolt Brecht

Nobody is interested in sweetness and light.

Hedda Hooper

Should we all confess our sins to one another we would laugh together at our lack of originality.

Kahlil Gibran

Many an attack of depression is nothing more than the expression of regret at having to be virtuous.

Wilhelm Stekhel

Many people think they're being charitable when they give away things they don't want.

Myrtle Reed

The only immorality is not to do what one has to do when one has to do it.

Jean Anouilh

It's hard to believe that a man is telling the truth when you know you would lie if you were in his place.

H L Mencken

The trouble with the rat race is that even if you win, you're still a rat.

Lily Tomlin

Penitence is remorse code.

John Crosbie

If we had no faults of our own, we would not take so much pleasure in noticing those of others.

La Rochefoucauld

A man who trusts nobody is apt to be the kind of man nobody trusts.

Harold Macmillan

A pessimist is a man who thinks all women are bad. An optimist is one who hopes they are.

Chauncey Depew

It takes a certain courage and a certain greatness to be truly base.

Jean Anouilh

Happiness is driving over a traffic warden's foot.

Kenny Everett

Any fool can tell the truth, but it requires a man of some sense to know how to lie well.

Samuel Butler

Censors are paid to have dirty minds.

John Trevelyan

Many men's idea of fidelity is not having more than one woman in their bed at a given time.

Jill Tweedle

I do not mind lying, but I hate inaccuracy.

Samuel Butler

We only admit our little faults to persuade others we have no great ones.

La Rochefoucauld

It's easier to cope with a bad conscience than a bad reputation.

Friedrich Nietzsche

If one tells the truth, one is sure, sooner or later, to be found out.

Oscar Wilde

Kill a man and you are a murderer. Kill millions of men and you are a conqueror. Kill everyone and you are a god.

Jean Rostand

He that first cries out 'Stop thief' is often he that has stolen the treasure.

William Congreve

Teamwork is always essential in a sales force. That way you always have someone to blame.

Donald Trump

There's no such thing as bravery, only degrees of fear.

John Wainwright

The idea of minding your own business is rubbish. Who could be so selfish?

Myrtle Barker

What isn't good for the beehive can't be good for the bees.

Marcus Aurelius

I always divide people into two groups: those who live by what they know to be a lie and those who live by what they believe, falsely, to be the truth.

Christopher Hampton

When one has a conscience, it is generally a bad one.

Eugene Ionesco

Being a hero is about the shortest-lived profession on earth.

Will Rogers

A lie can be half way round the world before the truth has got its boots on.

James Callaghan

What is moral is what you feel good after, and what is immoral is what you feel bad after.

Ernest Hemingway

A lawyer with his briefcase can steal more than a hundred men with guns.

Mario Puzo

It is absurd to divide people into good and bad. People are either charming or tedious.

Oscar Wilde

The great mass of people will more easily fall victim to a big lie than to a small one.

Adolf Hitler

No one gossips about other people's secret virtues.

Bertrand Russell

We all re-write our pasts to improve our present view of ourselves.

George Melly

When you say you agree to a thing in principle, you mean you haven't the slightest intention of carrying it out in practice.   *Spencer Tracy*

The golden rule is that there are no golden rules.
                                        George Bernard Shaw

FAMOUS LAST WORDS

If Mr Selwyn calls, let him in. If I'm alive I shall be very glad to see him, and if I'm not, he'll be very glad to see me.   *Lord Holland*

They couldn't hit an elephant at this dist . . .
                                        General Lord Sedgwick

Thank heaven the sun is gone in and I don't have to go out and enjoy it.   *Logan Smith*

Dying is a very dull, dreary affair. And my advice to you is to have nothing whatever to do with it.
                                        W Somerset Maugham

That was a great game of golf, fellers.   *Bing Crosby*

I've had 18 straight whiskies – I think that's the record.
                                        Dylan Thomas

It's a long time since I've drunk champagne.
                                        Anton Chekhov

I think I could eat one of Bellamy's veal pies.
                                        William Pitt the Younger

I'm dying with the help of too many physicians.

Peter the Great

Doctor, do you think it could have been the sausages?

Paul Claudel

I should never have switched from scotch to martinis.

Humphrey Bogart

I'm sorry to disappoint the vultures.   *Stephen Ward*

I'm getting better.   *D H Lawrence*

Everybody's got to die, but I always thought an
exception would be made in my case. Now what?

William Saroyan

You can keep the things of bronze and stone and give
me one man to remember me just once a year.

Damon Runyon

I don't have to forgive my enemies; I've had them all
shot.   *Ramon Narvaez*

So it has come at last, the distinguished thing.

Henry James

I feel nothing, apart from a certain difficulty in
continuing to exist.   *Bernard de Fontenelle*

Thank you, sister. May you be the mother of a bishop.

Brendan Behan

If this is dying, I don't think much of it.   *Lytton Strachey*

Either these curtains go or I do.   *Oscar Wilde*

That guy's gotta stop.   *James Dean*

Et tu, Brute?   *Julius Caesar*

Here am I, dying of a hundred good symptoms.
     Alexander Pope

Die, my dear doctor? That's the last thing I shall ever
do.   *Lord Palmerston*

I have been a most unconscionable time dying, but I
hope you will excuse it.   *King Charles II*

Does nobody understand me?   *James Joyce*

Don't pull down the blinds. I feel fine.   *Rudolph Valentino*

I am dying as fast as my enemies could wish and as
cheerfully as my friends could desire.   *David Hume*

I've never felt better.   *Douglas Fairbanks*

Such is life.   *Ned Kelly*

I'd rather be ski-ing than doing this.   *Stan Laurel*

I'm shot. I'm shot.   *John Lennon*

Kiss me, sweet wife, and I'll try to sleep a little.

Charles Stewart Parnell

If this is what viral pneumonia does to you, I really don't think I shall bother to have it again.

Dame Gladys Cooper

On the whole, I'd prefer to be in Philadelphia.

W C Fields

What an artist the world is losing in me.   **Nero**

Be sure you show the mob my head. It will be a long time before they see its like.

Georges Danton before being executed in the French Revolution

It is finished.   **Jesus Christ**

FOOD & DIET

If God meant us to eat peanut butter He would have given us Teflon gums.   **Robert Orpen**

Anything you have to acquire a taste for wasn't meant to be eaten.   **Eddie Murphy**

The best number for a dinner party is two: myself and a damn good head waiter.   **John Candy**

Don't eat too many almonds. They add weight to the breasts.   **Colette**

Never serve oysters in a month that has no pay cheque in it.
P J O'Rourke

Don't tell your friends about your indigestion. 'How are you' is a greeting, not a question. *Arthur Guiterman*

Don't let love interfere with your appetite.
Anthony Trollope

Life is too short to stuff a mushroom. *Shirley Conran*

A watermelon that breaks open by itself tastes better than one cut with a knife. *Hualing Nieh*

If people have to choose between friends and sandwiches, they'll choose sandwiches. *Lord Boyd-Orr*

Each year a healthy male bore consumes one and a half times his own weight in other people's patience.
John Updike

All the things I really like to do are either illegal, immoral or fattening. *Alexander Woollcott*

Manners is the noise you don't make eating soup.
Leonard Levinson

There is a vast difference between the savage and the civilised man, but it's never apparent to their wives until after breakfast. *Helen Rowland*

Every woman's dream is to be able to send a man out to the garden and tell him to stay there until the next meal.   *Virginia Graham*

There is no such thing as a little garlic.   *Arthur Baer*

The best way to keep milk from turning sour is to leave it in the cow.   *Kenny Everett*

Good mashed potatoes are one of the great luxuries of life, and I don't blame Elvis for eating them non-stop every night.   *Lindsey Bareham*

As for butter versus margarine, I trust cows more than chemists.   *Joan Gussow*

The best way to lose weight is to put the handle of the fridge two inches from the ground.   *Dawn French*

No man is lonely while eating spaghetti.   *Robert Morley*

The only thing that tastes exactly like butter is butter.
                                                Arthur Marshall

It wasn't the apple on the tree that caused the problem in the Garden of Eden, but the pair on the ground.
                                                        Anon

The golden rule when reading a menu in a restaurant is, if you can't pronounce it, you can't afford it.
                                                  Frank Muir

Eat, drink and be merry, for tomorrow ye diet.
William Gilmour

You don't have to lay an egg to know if it tastes good.
Pauline Kael

Never eat anything at one sitting that you can't lift.
Jim Henson

Love never dies of starvation, but often of indigestion.
Ninon de Lenclos

I'm president of the United States and I'm not going to eat any more broccoli.
George Bush in 1990

Eating cottage cheese is like kissing your sister.
Isabelle Lucas

Part of the secret of success in life is to eat what you want and let the food fight it out inside.
Mark Twain

Man cannot live by bread alone. He must also have peanut butter.
James Garfield

Just give me chocolate and nobody gets hurt.
T-shirt slogan

You could possibly get through life without knowing how to roast a chicken, but would you want to?
Nigella Lawson

If I can't have too many truffles I'll do without.
Colette

Cooking is like love. It should be entered into with
abandon or not at all. **Harriet van Horne**

When I was a child, the family menu consisted of two
choices: take it or leave it. **Buddy Hackett**

I am not a glutton. I am an explorer of food.
Erma Bombeck

Over-eating is the most worthy of sins. It neither
breaks up marriages nor causes any accidents.
Richard Gordon

I do not over-eat because my mother slapped me when
I was five. I over-eat because I'm a damned hog.
Dolly Parton

Terror is the word for facing a day with only 800
calories. **Helen Gurley Brown**

I've got my figure back after giving birth. Pity. I'd
hoped to get someone else's. **Caroline Quentin**

I always eat dessert first because life is so uncertain.
Robert Morley

A diet is a system of starving yourself to death so you
can live a little longer. **Totie Fields**

I told the doctor I had a terrible stomach problem. She
said, 'You have. It's bloody enormous.' **Jo Brand**

Always serve too much hot fudge sauce on hot fudge sundaes. It makes people overjoyed, and puts them in your debt.   *Judith Olney*

Everything you see I owe to spaghetti.   *Sophia Loren*

I fantasise about scientists discovering that lettuce is fattening.   *Erma Bombeck*

There are an awful lot of skinny people in the cemetery.
                                    Beverly Sills

Diets don't suit me. I got addicted to the menu.
                                      Mort Sahl

Never trust a thin cook.   *Charlotte Wright*

I am on a diet as my skin doesn't fit me any more.
                                   Erma Bombeck

His bark is worse than his bite if he's been eating garlic.
                                    Red Skelton

Is it progress if a cannibal uses a knife and fork?
                                   Stanislaus Lec

Never regret the fact that you're not immortal. Just imagine what your meat bills would be.   *Woody Allen*

Liz Taylor likes food so much she takes mayonnaise on her aspirins.   *Joan Rivers*

Businessmen attach an exaggerated importance to the
healing power of lunch.   *Christopher Fieldes*

All happiness depends on a leisurely breakfast.
                                  John Gunter

Stolen waters are sweet, and bread eaten in secret is
pleasant.   *The Bible*

Faith can move mountains . . . she's a pretty big girl.
                                  Graffiti

Self-denial is not a virtue; it is only the effect of
prudence on rascality.   *George Bernard Shaw*

An abstainer is a weak man who yields to the
temptation of denying himself a pleasure.
                                  Ambrose Bierce

The laziest man I ever met put popcorn in his
pancakes so they'd turn over by themselves.   *W C Fields*

She had the biggest overbite in history. She used to eat
a piece of toast and finish the outer edges first.
                                  Woody Allen

Eat what you like until you're five pounds overweight,
then lose ten pounds. Then, dear boy, start eating
again.   *Noel Coward*

I said to my son, 'Finish up all your meat and you'll be
just like Daddy'. Since then he only eats vegetables.
                                  Rodney Dangerfield

The last time I stepped on one of those 'I Speak Your Weight' machines it said 'One at a time, please!'

Jackie Gleason

I'm on a sea-food diet. Whenever I see food, I eat it.

Derek Davis

I've been on a constant diet for the last two decades. I've lost a total of 789 pounds. By all accounts, I should be hanging from a charm bracelet.

Erma Bombeck

I once went on a three-week diet . . . and lost 21 days.

Jack Leonard

My Uncle Charlie told me where milk comes from, but I still like it.

Hank Ketcham

I make a lot of jokes about vegetarians in my act but most of them don't have the strength to protest.

Ardal O'Hanlon

It was such a shame she grew up. And out.

Bette Davis on Shirley Temple

It doesn't matter to me that you haven't seen your navel in 25 years and that you can wear your stomach as a kilt. Just tell me you're happy.

Jennifer Saunders

Swallow razor blades if you want to sharpen your appetite.

Janet Rogers

GENERAL OBSERVATIONS

The greatest glory in living lies not in never falling, but in rising every time we fall.
Nelson Mandela

Not many people have the luck to consult a psychiatrist and come out on the winning side.
Richard Gordon

The worst music you're ever likely to hear in your life is what they play during a TV breakdown.
John Symons

The closest to perfection we ever get in life is when we fill out a job application form.
James Simpson

When a duty ceases to be a pleasure, it ceases to exist.
Norman Douglas

You can make more friends in two months by being interested in other people than you can in two years by trying to get other people interested in you.
Dale Carnegie

No one would listen to you talk if he didn't know it was his turn next.
Ed Howe

There are two golden rules for an orchestra: start together and finish together. The public doesn't give a damn about what goes on in between.
Sir Thomas Beecham

Some people can stay longer in an hour than others
can in a week.   *W D Howells*

Jogging is for people who aren't intelligent enough to
watch TV AM.   *Victoria Wood*

An intellectual is a man who says a simple thing in a
difficult way. An artist is a man who says a difficult
thing in a simple way.   *Charles Bukowski*

For an idea ever to be fashionable is ominous, since it
must afterwards be always old-fashioned.
                                                  George Santayana

The man who has to muck out the monkeys is rarely,
if ever, consulted when the architects roll up in their
limousines to sketch out the new monkey-house.
                                                  David Taylor

In my day there were things that were done and things
that were not done. And there was even a way of doing
things that were not done.   *Peter Ustinov*

The best way to capture a horse is to build a fence
around it.   *Emmylou Harris*

There is nothing in which people more betray their
character than in what they laugh at.
                                                  Wolfgang von Goethe

James Bond rules OOK.   *Graffiti*

Bad spellers of the world untie.   *Janet Rogers*

Immigration is the sincerest form of flattery.
                                    Herbert Prochnow

The ultimate indignity in a woman's life is to be given
a bedpan by a stranger who calls you by your first name.
                                    Maggie Kuhn

We love people who come right out and say what they
mean – provided they agree with us.   *Jilly Cooper*

Most human beings have an almost infinite capacity
for taking things for granted.   *Aldous Huxley*

The history of philosophy can be summed up as
follows.
Aristotle: To be is to do.
Sartre: To do is to be.
Sinatra: Dooby dooby dooby do.   *Graffiti*

There comes a dreadful moment in our lives when
foreign friends, whom we strongly urged to visit us,
actually do so.   *Virginia Graham*

Horse sense is the thing a horse has which keeps it
from betting on people.   *W C Fields*

It's a pity our ancestors didn't live long enough to see
how smart the modern generation is.   *Herbert Prochnow*

There is nothing more terrifying than to be alone with sheer time. Then the ghosts come crowding in. They can be very sinister, very mischievous, raising a thousand doubts in your mind about the people outside and their loyalty. Was your sacrifice worth the trouble? What would your life have been like if you hadn't got involved?   *Nelson Mandela*

If truth is beauty, how come no one has their hair done in the library?   *Lily Tomlin*

Every society honours its live conformists and its dead troublemakers.   *Mignon McLaughlin*

The more truth is shook, the more it shines.
                    Sir William Hamilton

Show me a good loser and I'll show you a loser.
                    Lawrie McMenemy

The dying process begins the minute we are born, but it accelerates during dinner parties.   *Carol Matthau*

Ninety-nine per cent of lawyers give the rest a bad name.   *Lily Tomlin*

Winter is the time of year when it gets late early.
                    Dan Crosbie

Einstein rules relatively OK.   *Graffiti*

It has long been an axiom of mine that the little things are infinitely the most important.   *Sir Arthur Conan Doyle*

When introducing people at social gatherings, hostesses mumble names as if they were dirty words.

Desmond Morris

Flatterers say things to your face that they wouldn't dare say behind your back.

Herbert Prochnow

When somebody says 'I hope you won't mind me telling you this,' it's pretty certain you will.

Sylvia Bremer

I don't know the difference between ignorance and apathy and I don't care.

Graffiti

Several excuses are always less convincing than one.

Aldous Huxley

We've got to take the atom bomb seriously. It's dynamite.

Samuel Goldwyn

One of the things that rarely turns out as it should in life is the car ahead of you.

Herbert Prochnow

The impossible we can do today. Miracles require advance notice.

Office notice

Once a woman becomes equal to man, she becomes his inferior.

Socrates

The opposite of talking isn't listening; it's waiting.

Fran Lebowitz

There are three guidelines for bureaucrats: when in charge, ponder. When in trouble, delegate. When in doubt, mumble. *James Boren*

I've never been to Alaska, but I know it's cold up there. *Michael Taylor*

Even a broken clock is right twice a day. *David Steel*

Cocaine isn't habit-forming. I should know: I've been using it for years. *Tallulah Bankhead*

A kleptomaniac is a man who helps himself because he can't help himself. *Herbert Prochnow*

Show me someone who never gossips and I'll show you someone who isn't interested in people. *Barbara Walters*

The man with toothache thinks everyone happy whose teeth are sound. *George Bernard Shaw*

The only time a fisherman tells the truth is when he calls other fishermen liars. *Bob Monkhouse*

Nothing much gets said at cocktail parties until a few couples leave. *George Burns*

Men sooner forget the death of their father than the loss of their possessions. *Machiavelli*

Once a job is fouled up, anything to improve it only makes it worse. *Arthur Bloch*

A change is as good as arrest.   *Billy Connolly*

I have a carefully worked out plan for doing the Christmas shopping. It's called panic.   *Paul Daniels*

A good scientific theory should be explicable to a barmaid.   *Ernest Rutherford*

You never realise how much furniture you've collected until you have to go to the loo in the dark.   *Denis Norden*

A man travels the world in search of what he needs and returns home to find it.   *George Moore*

Psychiatry's chief contribution to philosophy is the discovery that the toilet is the seat of the soul.   *Alexander Chase*

Whenever people agree with me I always feel I must be wrong.   *Oscar Wilde*

If we lawyers only took on cases in which we really believed, we'd go out of business in no time.   *Henry Cecil*

Where there is no imagination there is no horror.   *Sir Arthur Conan Doyle*

The test of a real comedian is whether you laugh at him before he opens his mouth.   *George Jean Nathan*

It is the mark of a good action that it appears
inevitable in retrospect. **Robert Louis Stevenson**

The surest way of losing one's dignity is to stand on it.
Lambert Jeffries

He that complies against his will,
Is of his own opinion still. **Samuel Butler**

History a distillation of rumour. **Thomas Carlyle**

I loathe people who keep dogs. They're cowards who
haven't got the guts to bite people themselves.
August Strindberg

In a real dark night of the soul it is always three
o'clock in the morning. **F Scott Fitzgerald**

Show me a man who has enjoyed his schooldays and
I'll show you a bully and a bore. **Robert Morley**

When you become famous you get to torture a higher
class of man than before. **Sharon Stone**

Art is not a mirror but a hammer. **John Grierson**

I wish I was what I used to be when I wished I was
what I am. **Anon**

Anger as soon as fed is dead. **Emily Dickinson**

Dyslexia rules KO. **Graffiti**

It's only the boring who are bored.   *W Somerset Maugham*

Even sharks need parasites.   *Ian Pattison*

I'll give you a definite maybe.   *Samuel Goldwyn*

Genius is 1% inspiration and 99% perspiration.
Thomas Edison

Man invented language in order to satisfy his deep
need to complain.   *Lily Tomlin*

I have finally come to the conclusion that a reliable set
of bowels is worth more to a man than any quantity of
brains.   *Josh Billings*

Friends aren't necessarily the people you like best, they
are merely the people who got there first.   *Peter Ustinov*

Practically anything you say will be amusing if you're
on all fours.   *P J O'Rourke*

A well-adjusted executive is one whose intake of pep
pills over-balances his consumption of tranquillisers
just enough to leave him sufficient energy for the
weekly visit to his psychiatrist.   *Arthur Motley*

I have yet to see any problem, however complicated,
which, when looked at in the right way, did not
become even more complicated.   *Paul Anderson*

Knowledge is power – if you know it about the right people. ***Ethel Watts Mumford***

There are some sacrifices which should not be demanded twice from any man, and one of them is listening to Brahms' Requiem. ***George Bernard Shaw***

One of the most difficult things to contend with in a hospital is the assumption on the part of the staff that because you have lost your gall bladder you have also lost your mind. ***Jean Kerr***

A bit of shooting makes you forget your troubles. ***Brendan Behan***

I have come to regard the law courts not as cathedrals but casinos. ***Richard Ingrams***

I would rather sit on a pumpkin and have it all to myself than to be crowded on a velvet cushion. ***Henry David Thoreau***

The misfortunes hardest to bear are those which never come. ***James Russell Lowell***

To apologise is to lay the foundation for a future offence. ***Ambrose Bierce***

Ideals are like items you pack in your luggage and take with you everywhere but never get to wear. ***William McIlvanney***

The things people discard tell more about them than the things they keep.   *Hilda Lawrence*

There are many who dare not kill themselves for fear of what the neighbours would say.   *Cyril Connolly*

Some are born great, some have greatness thrust upon them, and some hire PR officers.   *Daniel Boorstin*

Better be ignorant of a matter than half know it.
Publilius Syrus

Inner city council estates make you believe the world was really built in six days.   *Kathy Lette*

Liking oneself is often an acquired taste.   *Martin Amis*

Visitors, like fish, stink after three days.   *Proverb*

Happiness is a house without a telephone.   *Gay Byrne*

Everything is data. But data isn't everything.
Pauline Bart

Croquet is the polo of senility.   *Jimmy Cannon*

Competitions are for horses, not artists.   *Bela Bartok*

The more you know, the less you better.
Scottish proverb

When people say 'I'll let you know,' you know.
Laurence J Peter

The chief distinction of a diplomat is that he can say no in such a way that it sounds like yes.   *Lester Pearson*

Military intelligence is a contradiction in terms.
Spike Milligan

Plagiarists are generally thieves of bad gags.
Henny Youngman

To have a grievance is to have a purpose in life.
Eric Hoffer

No one can make us hate ourselves like an admirer.
Cyril Connolly

Nobody is born prejudiced against others, but everyone is born prejudiced in favour of himself.
David Stafford Clark

Anyone who can walk to the welfare office can walk to work.   *Al Capp*

Diplomacy is the art of letting someone else have your way.   *David Frost*

My breasts aren't actresses.
Liv Ullman refusing to do a nude scene in a movie

The thought of suicide is a good way of getting through many a bad night.   *Friedrich Nietzsche*

We need two kinds of acquaintances: one to complain to while we boast to the other.   *Logan Pearsall Smith*

A great deal of nonsense is talked about the dignity of work. Work is a drug that most people take to avoid the pangs of unmitigated boredom.

W Somerset Maugham

Science may carry us to Mars, but it will leave the earth, as ever, peopled by the inept. *Agnes Repplier*

The fascination of shooting as a sport depends entirely on whether you are on the right or wrong end of the gun. *P G Wodehouse*

If you can understand a contract, it must be legally unsound. *Lambert Jeffries*

A psychiatrist is a man you start talking to after you start talking to yourself. *Graffiti*

Manners are especially the need of the plain. The pretty can get away with anything. *Evelyn Waugh*

You might as well employ a boa constrictor for a tape measure as go to a lawyer for legal advice.

Oliver St John Gogarty

Anyone who needs 50,000 people a night to tell him they're all right, like we do, must have a bit missing.

Bono on U2

If you think squash is a competitive activity, try flower arranging. *Alan Bennett*

Sometimes we have to lose our minds to come to our senses.
Frederick Peris

The trouble with our generation is that it's all signpost and no destination.
Louis Kronenberger

The turning point in the history of western civilisation was reached with the invention of the electric guitar.
Leni Sinclair

Happy people are failures because they're on such good terms with themselves they don't give a damn.
Agatha Christie

The physician can bury his mistakes, but the architect can only advise his client to plant vines.
Frank Lloyd Wright

It's better to be quotable than honest.
Tom Stoppard

I wish I was as cocksure of anything as Tom Macaulay is of everything.
Lord Melbourne

We have to distrust each other. It's our only weapon against betrayal.
Tennessee Williams

Many an attack of depression is nothing but the expression of regret at having to be virtuous.
Wilhelm Stekhel

We cry when we are born. What follows is merely an attenuation of that cry.
Françoise Sagan

You never step into the same river twice.   *Heraclitus*

Basic research is what I'm doing when I don't know
what I'm doing.   *Bertrand Russell*

It is impossible to enjoy idling thoroughly unless one
has plenty of work to do.   *Jerome K Jerome*

People, like sheep, tend to follow a leader –
occasionally in the right direction.   *Alexander Chase*

It's fatal to be appreciated in one's own time.
Osbert Sitwell

The next best thing to being clever is being able to
quote someone who is.   *Mary Pettibone Poole*

Examiners, like lightning, never strike twice in the
same place.   *Richard Gordon*

Water, taken in moderation, cannot hurt anybody.
Mark Twain

There are very few people who don't become more
interesting when they stop talking.   *Mary Lowry*

We cherish our friends not for their ability to amuse
us, but for ours to amuse them.   *Evelyn Waugh*

The first mistake in public business is to be going into
it.   *Benjamin Franklin*

The place where optimism most flourishes is the
lunatic asylum.
Havelock Ellis

It is the tragedy of the world that no one knows what
he doesn't know, and the less a man knows, the more
sure he is that he knows everything.
Joyce Cary

I've never had a humble opinion. If you've got an
opinion, why be humble about it?
Joan Baez

Regret for the things we did can be tempered by time.
It's regret for the things we didn't do that is
inconsolable.
Sydney Harris

We tolerate shapes in human beings that would horrify
us if we saw them in a horse.
W R Inge

The amount of sleep required by the average person is
five minutes more.
Max Kauffmann

All dentists talk while they work. They have inherited
this from their professional ancestors, the barbers.
Mark Twain

A hen is only an egg's way of making another egg.
Samuel Butler

No artist is ahead of his time. He is his time. It's just
that everyone else is behind it.
Martha Graham

The human brain starts working the moment you're
born and doesn't stop until you stand up to speak in
public.
George Jessel

To his dog, every man is Napoleon. Hence the
constant popularity of dogs.   *Aldous Huxley*

Every man sees in his relations a series of grotesque
caricatures of himself.   *H L Mencken*

Art for art's sake makes no more sense than gun for
gun's sake.   *W Somerset Maugham*

The first twenty years of life contain the whole of
experience. The rest is observation.   *Graham Greene*

The only way to succeed is to make people hate you.
That way they remember you.   *Joseph von Sternberg*

There's no female Mozart because there's no female
Jack the Ripper.   *Camille Paglia*

What you have become is the price you paid to get
what you used to want.   *Mignon McLaughlin*

Researchers have proved that liars can control other
parts of their body but generally forget about their feet.
A liar can never stand still.   *Diana Dors*

The world is moving so fast these days that the man
who says it can't be done is usually interrupted by the
man doing it.   *Elbert Hubbard*

If many remedies are suggested for a disease, it means
the disease is incurable.   *Anton Chekhov*

The world is made up of people who never quite get into the first team, and who just miss the prizes at the flower show.   *David Broder*

My pessimism extends to the point of even suspecting the sincerity of the pessimists.   *Jean Rostand*

The final delusion is the belief that one has lost all delusions.   *Maurice Chapelain*

Class is when they run you out of town and you look like you're leading the parade.   *Bill Battie*

The past is history, the future is a mystery and the present is a gift. That's why we call it the present.
                                        Ruth Cassell

An interesting life is better not lived.   *Chinese proverb*

Don't vote. The government always gets in.
                                     Adrian Edmondson

Tyranny is always better organised than freedom.
                                        Charles Peguy

Conservatives believe in reform, but not yet.   *Anon*

History is bunk.   *Henry Ford*

Policemen are numbered in case they get lost.
                                       Spike Milligan

Initiative is successful disobedience.   *John Fenton*

A fool and his words are soon parted.   *William Shenstone*

A loafer always has the correct time.   *Kin Hubbard*

Better a wise madness than a foolish sanity.
Huck Finneral

If you behave like an artist, you'll never be one.
Mary Astor

There are no ugly women, only lazy ones.
Helena Rubinstein

It's a sad woman who buys her own perfume.
Lena Jeger

A bore is a person not interested in you.
Mary Pettibone Poole

Innocence ends when one is stripped of the delusion
that one likes oneself.   *Joan Didion*

I have nothing against undertakers personally but I
wouldn't like one of them to bury my sister.
Jessica Mitford

Nobody knows anything.   *William Goldman*

Surely nothing could be that funny.
*George Melly after Mick Jagger told him his wrinkles were
merely 'laughter lines'*

HOLLYWOOD

Rudolph Valentino had the acting talent of the average wardrobe.
Clyde Jeavons

I'm not very good at being me. That's why I adore acting so much.
Deborah Kerr

Being a celebrity is a no-win situation. If you get along with your co-star you're having an affair; if you don't you're having a feud.
Barbra Streisand

Movies are so rarely great art that if we can't appreciate the great trash, we have very little reason to be interested.
Pauline Kael

Comedy is like a soufflé: if it gets overdone, it crashes. It's like music – you hear the beat in your head.
Goldie Hawn

Hollywood is the only place in the world where an amicable divorce means each one gets 50% of the publicity.
Lauren Bacall

I ask for the money I want and they pay it – it's that simple.
Harrison Ford

Actors don't believe in illness. So we don't get ill.
Donald Sinden

What you get is a living. What you give is a life.
Lillian Gish

I never looked through a keyhole without finding someone was looking back.   *Judy Garland*

The fact that I became famous gives me a form of happiness, but it's only temporary. It's like caviar: it's nice, but I don't want caviar every night.   *Marilyn Monroe*

There's nothing better than to know I can be taking a bath at home and at the same time someone is watching me in Brazil.   *Barbra Streisand*

Show me an actress who isn't a personality and I'll show you a woman who isn't a star.   *Katharine Hepburn*

When I'm lying drunk at an airport, the press call me Irish . . . but when I win an Oscar, I'm classified as British.   *Brenda Fricker*

I never remember anyone's name. Where do you think the *dahling* thing started?   *Zsa Zsa Gabor*

Virtue may be its own reward, but it has no sale at the box office.   *Mae West*

It was a dull week in Hollywood when my engagement wasn't announced to one man or another.
Tallulah Bankhead

Five stages in the life of an actor: 1. Who's Mary Astor? 2. Get me Mary Astor. 3. Get me a Mary Astor type. 4. Get me a young Mary Astor. 5. Who's Mary Astor?
Mary Astor

Why should people go out and pay money to see bad films when they can stay home and see bad television for nothing?
Samuel Goldwyn

I'm one of those people who imagined I could direct Frank Sinatra. It's a bit like being one of the girls who thought they'd get Howard Hughes to marry them.
Robert Aldrich

Julie Andrews has that wonderful British strength that makes you wonder why they lost India.
Moss Hart

Brigitte Bardot is just the kind of girl to take home to mother – if you want to give her a heart attack.
Tony Crawley

I'm a very good actor. I played all those love scenes with Phyllis Calvert and we didn't like each other very much.
Stewart Granger

You're doing it the wrong way round, my boy. You're a star and you don't know how to act.
Cecil Hardwicke to Richard Chamberlain

If people don't sit at Charlie Chaplin's feet, he goes out and stands where they are sitting.
Herman Mankiewicz

Robert Redford is even a star in the shower. No water spray would dare give him hassle. The water would never be too hot or too cold, and the eggs at breakfast would always come out of the pan perfect.
Paul Newman

The width of a Hollywood smile in my direction is commensurate with how much my last picture grossed.

Marlon Brando

Charlton Heston is good at portraying arrogance and ambition. But in the same way that a dwarf is good at being short.

Rex Harrison

Most actors are like the very young. They long to rebel and conform at the same time. Now they do this by defying the public and copying each other.

Lorne Greene

Hollywood producers are low grade individuals with the morals of a goat, the artistic integrity of a slot machine, and the manners of a floorwalker with delusions of grandeur.

Raymond Chandler

He looks as if his idea of fun would be to find a nice damp grave and sit in it.

Richard Winnington on Paul Henreid

Susan Hayward spoke in a voice like black coffee without sugar.

Tom Wiseman

Jennifer Lopez has as much star power as a broken lightbulb.

Philip Molloy

After they realised *Easy Rider* was going to be a hit, the Columbia executives stopped shaking their heads in incomprehension and started nodding them in incomprehension.

Peter Fonda

Floating in his pool, Charles Laughton was the reverse of an iceberg: 90% of him was visible. *Peter Ustinov*

I knew Daniel Day-Lewis before he was Irish.
Stephen Frears

It took longer to draw up one of Mary Astor's contracts than it did to make her pictures.
Samuel Goldwyn

Otto Preminger is really Martin Bormann in elevator shoes with a facelift by a blindfolded plastic surgeon in Luxembourg. *Billy Wilder*

Rudolph Valentino's first marriage lasted a day. That's about average for Hollywood. *Lupe Velez*

My biggest fear is the 100% performance . . . because after that the only way is down. *Glenda Jackson*

No, Jack Nicholson isn't sexy any more. In fact he wouldn't look out of place in a DIY store on a Thursday afternoon, availing of the OAP's discount.
Ciara Dwyer

I always wanted to be a movie star. I thought it meant being famous and having breakfast in bed. I didn't know you had to be up at 4 am. *June Allyson*

There are only three ages for women in Hollywood: Babe, District Attorney and Driving Miss Daisy.
Goldie Hawn

When someone follows you all the way to the shop
and watches you buy toilet roll, you know your life has
changed.   *Jennifer Aniston*

If Robert de Niro puts on weight for a part they call it
artistic dedication; if I do it's called letting myself go.
                                            Brenda Fricker

The more flesh you show in Hollywood, the higher up
the ladder you go.   *Kim Basinger*

Scratch an actor and you'll find an actress.
                                            Dorothy Parker

Joan Crawford is like that old joke about Philadelphia.
First prize, four years with her; second prize, *eight*.
                                            Franchot Tone

Liz Taylor's getting married again. By now she must
regret she didn't buy a time-share in Niagara Falls.
                                            Johnny Carson

I never said actors were cattle. All I said was that they
should be *treated* like cattle.   *Alfred Hitchcock*

I'm not really Henry Fonda. Nobody could have that
much integrity.   *Henry Fonda*

Show business is worse than dog eat dog. It's 'dog
won't return other dog's phone calls'.   *Woody Allen*

Does the word nightmare mean anything to you?
                                      James Woods on Sean Young

Cash And Cary.
Newspaper headline on the wedding of Cary Grant and super-rich Barbara Hutton.

Zsa Zsa Gabor has discovered the secret of perpetual middle age.
John Huston

Douglas was so impressed with the script, he asked if Mr Homer had written any other ones.
Russian radio station DJ on Kirk Douglas after he had signed for 'Ulysses'

He delivers every line with a monotonous tenor bark as if addressing an audience of deaf Eskimos.
Michael Billington on Peter O'Toole's performance of 'Macbeth'

I had no real ambition about acting, but I knew there had to be something better than the bloody chemist's shop.
Glenda Jackson

Ginger Rogers did everything that Fred Astaire did. She just did it backwards and in high heels.
Linda Ellerbee

If someone were to come from another planet and see the world through movies, they'd think it was populated by white men in their 30s who shoot a lot.
Bonnie Bedelia on violence in modern movies

All they ever did for me at MGM was change my leading men and the water in my pool.
Esther Williams

Cary Grant was an aloof, remote person intent on being Cary Grant playing Cary Grant playing Cary Grant.

Frances Farmer

Culturally and creatively, Jennifer Lopez is about as interesting as overheated meringue.

Barbara Ellen

Sometimes I have this feeling that I'd just like to walk down the street naked and leave it all behind.

Kim Basinger

Pierce Brosnan is so laid back you almost want to check him for a pulse.

Ciara Dwyer

I've done everything in the theatre except marry the property man.

Fanny Brice

I suppose I'm fortunate that all of me looks as if it was assembled in the same factory.

Michelle Pfeiffer

I once played Cher's dog on TV.

Teri Garr

I used to play a lot of lab assistants. I'd be the guy running in, yelling 'The place is on fire'. I'd come in, go out and that was it. I never got shot or died. If that had happened, I would have gotten more screen time than average . . . I did a *Francis the Talking Mule* picture once.

Clint Eastwood

I got my first part because I could belch on cue.

Charles Bronson

Buñuel cast me in *Viridiana* because he had been
impressed by a previous performance of mine as a
corpse.
Fernando Rey

Joan Collins has all the assurance of someone dealing
herself a fifth ace in a card game with children.
Louis Stanley

Even in his twenties, George Sanders had a face which
looked as though he had rented it out on a long lease.
David Niven

I'd hire the devil himself if he gave me a good story.
Samuel Goldwyn

It's very difficult being married to Joan of Arc.
Roger Vadim on Jane Fonda

Who can forget Mel Gibson in *Hamlet*? Much as we
try.
Harry Andrews

Joseph Cotton treats movie-making not so much as a
craft but rather a well-dressed social occasion.
Robert Aldrich

Her delivery of lines is rather like a grade-school pupil
asking to be excused to go to the bathroom.
John Simon on Ali MacGraw in 'Love Story'

Hollywood is the only place in the world where you
can wake up and hear the birds coughing in the trees.
Joe Frisco

You can see Sean Connery with a woman of twenty or thirty in films these days, but if you were to put a woman in her sixties with a young man, then the story has to be about *that*.   ***Demi Moore***

Part of the $10 million I've made in my career went for gambling, part for horses and part for women. The rest I spent foolishly.   ***George Raft***

You can get too easily seduced by Hollywood. The sun fries your brain, you get a couple of awards . . . and before you know it, you want a Rolls Royce.
                    James Woods

Acting saved me from an asylum, no doubt about it.
                    Mia Farrow

I aspire to be terrifically boring.   ***Jodie Foster***

I lived below the official American poverty line until I was 31.   ***Dustin Hoffman***

I saw what happened to Elvis Presley, which is why I never wanted to be a star in the first place.   ***Goldie Hawn***

The important thing in acting is to be able to laugh and cry. If I have to cry, I think of my sex life. If I have to laugh, I think of my sex life.   ***Glenda Jackson***

Popular icons have the kind of chic that Marxist revolutionaries had in the 60s. Arnold Schwarzenneger has become the new Che Guevara.   ***Toby Young***

Acting has never done anything for me except
encourage my vanity and provoke my arrogance.
Candice Bergen

I do a job. I get paid. I go home.   **Maureen Stapleton**

Acting is a way of living out one's insanity.
Isabelle Huppert

I don't understand acting except when I'm doing it.
And sometimes not even then.   **Nastassja Kinski**

An actress is someone with no ability, who sits around
waiting to go on alimony.   **Jackie Stallone**

Hollywood is a place that attracts people with huge
holes in their souls.   **Julia Phillips**

Hollywood is a town that doesn't just want you to fail
– it wants you to *die*.   **Jerry Katzenberg**

I identify with the strength of Frances Farmer, the
weakness of Vivien Leigh, the loneliness of Judy
Garland . . . and the attitude of Don Corleone.
Wendy James

I try to get away with as much as possible without
people laughing at me.   **Brian de Palma**

You don't have to kill a king to play Macbeth.
Michelle Pfeiffer

Failures are inevitable. Unfortunately, in film they live forever: and they're 40 feet high and 20 feet wide.

Harrison Ford

I turned Hamlet down because it was going to take up too much of my drinking time. **Richard Harris**

If I had cast Ronald Reagan as the presidential candidate in *The Best Man* it would have sated his appetite for the presidency and we'd all have been much better off. **Gore Vidal**

Mickey Rourke is a fine actor with an unerring knack for choosing the wrong movies. **Peter Travers**

Jayne Mansfield squealed out loud on the set and said she had a terrific idea. The director stared at her, then said: 'Treat it gently, dear. It's in a strange place'.

Tony Randall

A happy hunting ground for third-rate minds with boundless ambition, impenetrable hides, and an unquenchable thirst for money.

Barry Norman on Hollywood

I used to work for a living; then I became an actor.

Roger Moore

Actors marrying actors play a dangerous game. They're always fighting over the mirror. **Burt Reynolds**

After Arnold Schwarzenegger, Dolph Lundgren is a bit of a disappointment. At least Arnold looks as if he comes supplied with batteries. **Adam Mars-Jones**

Tom Selleck is the biggest boy scout in America.
John Hillerman

She's silicon from the knees up.
George Masters on Raquel Welch

To bring a sense of perfection to Hollywood is to go bagging tigers with a fly swatter. **Ben Hecht**

Audrey Hepburn is the patron saint of anorexics.
Orson Welles

They asked Jack Benny if he would do something for the Actors' Orphanage, so he shot both his parents and moved in. **Bob Hope**

I can sing as well as Fred Astaire can act. **Burt Reynolds**

It's a great help for a man to be in love with himself. For an actor, however, it is absolutely essential.
Robert Morley

The Cannes Film Festival is like Butlins on acid.
Frank Clarke

The Russians love Brooke Shields because her eyebrows remind them of Brezhnev. **Robin Williams**

The Academy Awards – a gold rush in dinner jackets.

Boris Morros

I have a love interest in every one of my films – a gun.

Arnold Schwarzenegger

Peter O'Toole was so catastrophic in *Macbeth* that a departing first-nighter was heard to remark to his wife, 'I'll bet the dog got sick in the car.' *Hugh Leonard*

Actors are usually awful at playing drunks. Robert Newton was good at it, but then it was usually for real.

Jeffrey Bernard

If that child had been born in the Middle Ages she would have been burned at the stake as a witch.

Lionel Barrymore on Margaret O'Brien

All I ever got from Hollywood was three lousy ex-husbands. *Ava Gardner*

Working in Hollywood gives you a certain expertise in the field of prostitution. *Jane Fonda*

Bogey's a helluva nice guy until 11.30 pm. After that he thinks he's Bogart. *Dave Chasen*

A day away from Tallulah Bankhead is like a week in the country. *Howard Dietz*

The nicest thing I can say about Frances Farmer is that she's unbearable. *William Wyler*

Surely no one but a mother could have loved Bette
Davis at the height of her career.   *Brian Aherne*

There's nothing the matter with Hollywood that a
good earthquake wouldn't cure.   *Moss Hart*

I started out as a lousy actress, and I've remained one.
Brigitte Bardot

It's better to appear in a good commercial in Japan
than a bad movie in America.   *Valerie Kaprisky*

Broderick Crawford's face resembled an aerial view of
the Ozarks.   *Hugh Leonard*

I've played bad women and wicked women and they
don't pay. If you play them too well, people hate you.
Simone Signoret

A painter paints, a musician plays, a writer writes . . .
but a movie actor *waits*.   *Mary Astor*

My mother was against me being an actress – until I
introduced her to Frank Sinatra.   *Angie Dickinson*

To heck with the natural look. Where would Marilyn
Monroe be if she'd clung to the colour God gave her?
We'd have a movie called *Gentlemen Prefer Mousey
Brown Hair*.   *Adair Lara*

I have been very rich, very beautiful, much adulated,
very famous . . . and very unhappy.   *Brigitte Bardot*

The best thing I own is the knife from *Fatal Attraction*. I hung it in my kitchen. It's my way of saying: 'Don't mess with me'.

Glenn Close

The price of fame? Every time I went on a date, I'd end up bringing 17 bodyguards with me.

Sylvester Stallone

Some communist – she travels by Rolls Royce.

Robert Duvall on Vanessa Redgrave

It wasn't an iceberg that sank the *Titanic* – it was Kate Winslet's weight.

Jay Leno

Let's face it: Billy Wilder at work is two people – Mr Hyde and Mr Hyde.

Harry Kurnitz

Celebrity is bestial. It is the worst type of karma because of the huge solitude it brings. You're like a gazelle that finds itself straying from the flock. And soon your path is cut off by lions.

Brad Pitt

IRONIES

Good sense about trivialities is better than nonsense about things that matter.

Max Beerbohm

Time enough to think of the future when you haven't any future to think of.

George Bernard Shaw

A new idea is delicate. It can be killed by a sneer or a yawn. It can be stabbed to death by a quip and worried to death by a frown on the right man's brow.

Charles Brower

The main reason men oppose progress isn't because they hate it, but rather that they love inertia.

Elbert Hubbard

Too often the opportunity knocks, but by the time you push back the chain, unhook the two locks and shut off the burglar alarm . . . it's too late.   **Rita Coolidge**

Strike while the irony is hot.   **Don Quinn**

Those who make the worst use of their time are the first to complain of its brevity.   **Jean de La Bruyère**

One man's wage rise is another man's price increase.

Harold Wilson

Progress is man's ability to complicate simplicity.

Thor Heyerdahl

I guess I should warn you. If I turn out to be particularly clear, you've probably misunderstood what I've said.   **Alan Greenspan**

An unbiased opinion is absolutely valueless.   **Oscar Wilde**

Any study of economies reveals invariably that the best time to buy something was last year.   **Marty Allen**

Being powerful is like being a lady. If you have to tell people you are, you aren't.

Jesse Carr

The unfortunate need people who will be kind to them; the prosperous need people to be kind to.

Aristotle

Man is still the most extraordinary computer of all.

John F Kennedy

It is better to lose the saddle than the horse.

Proverb

The minority is always right.

Henrik Ibsen

There are two times in a man's life when he should not speculate: when he can't afford it, and when he can.

Mark Twain

We're overpaying him, but he's worth it.

Samuel Goldwyn

The trouble with the profit system is that it's always been highly unprofitable to most people.

Elwyn White

A radical is a man with both feet planted firmly in the air.

Franklin D Roosevelt

Liberals understand everything expect people who don't understand *them*.

Lenny Bruce

When you're most successful is when you're most vulnerable: that's when you make your biggest mistakes.

Roger Foster

Pain is the root of knowledge.   *Simone Weil*

What you get free costs too much.   *Jean Anouilh*

LIFE'S VAGARIES

One machine can do the work of fifty ordinary men.
No machine can do the work of one extraordinary
man.   *Elbert Hubbard*

Most of one's life is one prolonged effort to prevent
oneself thinking.   *Aldous Huxley*

History teaches us that men and nations behave wisely
once they have exhausted all other alternatives.
     Abba Eban

It's not catastrophes or murders, deaths and diseases
that kill us. It's the way people look and laugh, and
run up the steps of buses.   *Virginia Woolf*

Bores bore each other too, but it never seems to teach
them anything.   *Don Marquis*

Almost everybody is born a genius and buried an idiot.
     Charles Bukowski

It's not enough to succeed. Others must fail.   *Gore Vidal*

When one has been threatened with a great injustice,
one accepts a smaller one as a favour.   *Jane Carlyle*

After three days men grow weary of a wench, a guest, and rainy weather.   *Benjamin Franklin*

Many people divide life into two parts: before their gall bladder operation and after it.   *Roy Boulting*

If only we'd stop trying to be happy we could have a pretty good time.   *Edith Wharton*

Man is ready to die for an idea provided it is not quite clear to him.   *Paul Eldridge*

Life is the art of drawing sufficient conclusions from insufficient premises.   *Ralph Butler*

The only way to prevent what is past is to put a stop to it before it happens.   *Sir Boyle Roche*

If we can't be our brother's keeper, let us at least not be his destroyer.   *John F Kennedy*

Giving up smoking is easy. I've done it hundreds of times.   *Mark Twain*

Less is only more when more is no good.   *Frank Lloyd Wright*

Television is for appearing on, not looking at.   *Noel Coward*

It is a good rule in life never to apologise. The right sort of people do not want apologies, and the wrong sort take a mean advantage of them.   *P G Wodehouse*

As long as I have a want, I have a reason for living.
Satisfaction is death.   *George Bernard Shaw*

There's no end to what you can accomplish if you
don't care who gets the credit.   *Florence Luscomb*

Half the misery in the world is caused by ignorance.
The other half is caused by knowledge.   *Bonar Thompson*

Once inside the airport terminal you will find a board
on which all flights but the one you were hoping to
meet are listed.   *Robert Morley*

If automation keeps up, man will atrophy all his limbs
but the push button finger.   *Frank Lloyd Wright*

When someone sings his own praises, he always gets
the tune too high.   *Mary Waldrip*

People in a temper often say a lot of silly, terrible
things that they really mean.   *Penelope Gilliatt*

We have stopped believing in progress. What progress
that is!   *Jorge Luis Borges*

A girl whose cheeks are covered with paint
Has an advantage with me over one whose ain't.
          Ogden Nash

Almost all crime is due to the repressed desire for
aesthetic expression.   *Evelyn Waugh*

If you can't beat 'em, nuke 'em.   *Graffiti*

A virus is only doing its job.   *David Cronenberg*

If two men on the same job agree all the time, then
one of them is useless. If they disagree all the time,
then both are useless.   *Darryl F Zanuck*

If A is success in life, A = X + Y + Z. Work is X, play
is Y, and Z is keeping your mouth shut.   *Albert Einstein*

Dying for an idea doesn't make as much sense as
letting the idea die.   *Wyndham Lewis*

In the long run, spoon-feeding teaches us nothing but
the shape of the spoon.   *E M Forster*

People who are waiting for you stand out far less
clearly than people you are waiting for.   *Jean Giraudoux*

In three words I can sum up everything I've learned
about life: it goes on.   *Robert Frost*

If a doctor or nurse uses the phrase, 'This won't hurt a
bit', be sure to ask to whom they're referring.
                                  Stephen Leacock

If not the best of all possible worlds, this is certainly
the most amusing.   *William Archer*

Business is often about killing your favourite children
to allow others to succeed.   *Sir John Harvey Jones*

It's a funny old world. In fact a man is lucky if he gets out of it alive.   *W C Fields*

It is not certain that everything in life is uncertain.
                                                              Blaise Pascal

Men love war because it's the one thing that stops people laughing at them.   *John Fowles*

If you send Christmas cards too early it looks as if you are simply soliciting cards in return. If you send them too late it more resembles a panic response than a message of goodwill.   *Oliver Pritchett*

Punctuality is the virtue of the bored.   *Evelyn Waugh*

People start going to psychiatrists when they're slightly cracked and continue until they're totally broke.   *Anon*

There was never an age in which useless knowledge was more important to us than our own.   *Charles Joad*

The next war will be fought with atom bombs and the one after that with spears.   *Harold Urey*

One of the privileges of the great is to witness catastrophes from a terrace.   *Jean Giraudoux*

The follies which a man most regrets in his life are those which he didn't commit when he had the opportunity.   *Helen Rowland*

Audiences like their blues singers to be miserable.
Janis Joplin

All the things one has forgotten scream for help in dreams.
Elias Canetti

Man is the only animal that can remain on friendly terms with the victims he intends to eat until he eats them.
Samuel Butler

Possessions are generally diminished by possession.
Friedrich Nietzsche

The search for happiness is one of the chief sources of unhappiness.
Eric Hoffer

Half our life is spent trying to find something to do with the time we've rushed through life trying to save.
Will Rogers

When the plane you're on is late, the one you have to transfer to is on time.
Francis O'Carroll

I have made it a rule never to smoke more than one cigarette at a time.
Mark Twain

When one realises that life is worthless, he either commits suicide or travels.
Edward Dahlberg

We have to believe in free will. We've got no choice.
Isaac Bashevis Singer

There are two kinds of statistics: the kind you look up
and the kind you make up.   *Rex Stout*

For every person spoiled by success, there are a
thousand spoiled by failure.   *Lambert Jeffries*

I am firm. You are obstinate. He is a pig-headed fool.
                                    Katharine Whitehorn

The becoming of man is the history of the exhaustion
of his possibilities.   *Susan Sontag*

My guess is that 80% of the human race goes through
life without having a single original thought.
                                           H L Mencken

There are worse things in life than death. Have you
ever spent an evening with an insurance salesman?
                                           Woody Allen

Nothing is so silly as the expression of a man being
complimented.   *Andre Gide*

What the film business really needs is some new clichés.
                                        Samuel Goldwyn

Life is a tragedy seen in close-up, but a comedy in
long-shot.   *Charlie Chaplin*

The trouble with our time is that the future isn't what
it used to be.   *Paul Valery*

Everybody is ignorant, except on different subjects.

Will Rogers

The difference between persistence and obstinacy is that one comes from a strong will and the other from a strong won't.

Anon

The trouble with the world is that the stupid are cocksure and the intelligent are full of doubt.

Bertrand Russell

An ugly life is still preferable to a beautiful funeral.

Katharine Hepburn

Medicine has now advanced so much that it's almost impossible for a doctor to find anything all right about a person.

H L Mencken

The only thing your friends will never forgive you for is your happiness.

Albert Camus

Golf to me seems to be an arduous way to go for a walk. I prefer to take the dogs out.

Princess Anne

Life is a gamble at terrible odds. If it was a bet you wouldn't take it.

Tom Stoppard

If there's one thing hypocrites hate, it's hypocrisy.

Jack Rosenthal

An idea isn't responsible for the people who believe in it.

Don Marquis

Cars are almost foolproof today, except for the one behind the wheel.   *Bill McMahon*

A 'few' people at a party is always twice as many as you bargained for.   *Spike Hughes*

Many people are more afraid of the *word* cancer than the disease itself.   *Norman Mailer*

Many of our daydreams would darken into nightmares if there were any danger of their coming true.
Logan Pearsall Smith

Nostradamus was an optimist.   *Graffiti*

Depression is when your get-up-and-go just got up and went.   *Anon*

There are two tragedies in life. One is not to get your heart's desire. The other is to get it.   *George Bernard Shaw*

Housework is something you do that nobody notices – until you don't do it.   *Joyce Jillson*

The future will one day be the present and will seem as unimportant as the present does now.
W Somerset Maugham

From the day she weighs 140 pounds, the chief excitement in a woman's life consists in spotting women who are fatter than she is.   *Helen Rowland*

As soon as doctors announce that a deadly disease can be cured, nature provides another one. *Henry Cecil*

I am never less alone than when alone. *Cicero*

We're not here for a long time. We're here for a good time. *Graffiti*

He who is known for being an early riser may sleep till noon. *William Howells*

It's better to be black than gay because when you're black you don't have to tell your mother. *Charles Pierce*

Life is like a B-movie. You don't want to leave in the middle of it, but you don't want to see it again either. *Ted Turner*

There are three ingredients in the good life: learning, earning and yearning. *Christopher Morley*

However big the fool, there's always a bigger one to admire him. *Nicolas Boileau*

Man's main task in life is to give birth to himself. *Erich Fromm*

There is no cure for birth and death save to enjoy the interval. *George Santayana*

The third-rate mind is only happy when it is thinking with the majority. The second-rate mind is only happy when it is thinking with the minority, and the first-rate mind is only happy when it is thinking. *A A Milne*

Hostility is expressed in a number of ways. One is laughter. *Katie Millett*

Perfection has one grave defect. It is apt to be dull. *W Somerset Maugham*

The more you find out about life, the uglier everything seems. *Frank Zappa*

The thought that we're enduring the unendurable is one of the things that keep us going. *Molly Haskell*

If you can get through the twilight, you'll live through the night. *Dorothy Parker*

Life is a long rehearsal for a play that's never produced. *Micháel MacLiammóir*

One is not born a woman. One becomes a woman. *Simone de Beauvoir*

The trouble with facts is that there are so many of them. *Samuel Crothers*

People are never convinced of the seriousness of your suffering, except by your death. *Albert Camus*

One of the saddest things about life is the fact that the only thing one can do for 8 hours a day is work. You can't eat or drink or make love for 8 hours.

William Faulkner

The height of cleverness is being able to conceal it.

La Rochefoucauld

Ask yourself whether you are happy and you cease to be so.

John Stuart Mill

The saying that beauty is only skin deep is a skin deep saying.

Herbert Spencer

To do two things at once is to do neither.

Publilius Syrus

Life is a choice between two wrong answers.

Sharyn McCrumb

Graveyards are full of inexpendable people.

Kathleen Watkins

It's easier to forgive an enemy than to forgive a friend.

William Blake

In this life you have to take the bad with the worst.

Anon

An existentialist swims with the tide, but faster.

Quentin Crisp

The best time to buy a used car is when it's new.

Bob Monkhouse

Life is a version of post-natal depression.   *Graffiti*

If I had my life to live over again I'd make all the same mistakes, only sooner.   *Tallulah Bankhead*

The more people want something, the more they think other people want it.   *Mary Webb*

There's no door in life that doesn't open for you that another one doesn't close.   *Cybill Shepherd*

For most men, life is a search for the proper manila envelope in which to get themselves filed.
          Clifton Fadiman

We spend our lives killing time and then time kills us.
          Herbert Spencer

The best way of forgetting how you think you feel is to concentrate on what you know you know.   *Mary Stewart*

That men do not learn very much from the lessons of history is the most important of all the lessons history has to teach us.   *Herman Hupfeld*

The survivors of a nuclear attack would envy the dead.
          Nikita Khrushchev

A rattlesnake that doesn't bite teaches you nothing.
          Jessamyn West

Prison won't work unless we start sending a better class of people there.   *Laurence J Peter*

Every one of us is sentenced to solitary confinement inside our own skins for life. *Tennessee Williams*

Success has a hundred fathers, but failure is an orphan. *William Goldman*

Life is a party, but you arrive after it's started and leave before it's finished. *Elsa Maxwell*

We joined the navy to see the world and what did we see? We saw the sea. *Irving Berlin*

The trouble with telling a good story is that it usually reminds the other fellow of a dull one. *Sid Caesar*

The only interesting answers are those which destroy the questions. *Susan Sontag*

Enemies are not those who hate us, but rather those whom we hate. *Peter Ustinov*

Refusing to have an opinion is a way of having one. *Luigi Pirandello*

He that leaveth nothing to chance will do few things ill, but he will do very few things. *Lord Halifax*

The least pain in our little finger gives us more concern and uneasiness than the destruction of millions of our fellow beings. *William Hazlitt*

It's a mad world, but I can never decide which side of the asylum wall is the inside. *Douglas Home*

Lovers of humanity generally hate people. *Roy Campbell*

Sleep is the best cure for insomnia. *W C Fields*

If you think you are not conceited, it means you're very conceited indeed. *C S Lewis*

There's no terror in a bang, only in the anticipation of it. *Alfred Hitchcock*

Polite conversation is rarely either. *Fran Lebowitz*

To love oneself is the beginning of a lifelong romance. *Oscar Wilde*

Most success comes from ignoring the obvious. *Trevor Holdsworth*

Flattery never seems absurd
The flattered always take your word. *John Gay*

We are tomorrow's past. *Mary Webb*

The first pull of the curtains always sends them in the wrong direction. *Fran Lebowitz*

Crazy paving isn't all it's cracked up to be. *Graffiti*

I would have thought that the knowledge that you are going to be leapt on by half a dozen congratulatory but sweaty team-mates would be an inducement not to score a goal at soccer.   *Arthur Marshall*

To gain a greater understanding of mankind, break the word into two parts: 'mank' and 'ind'.   *Rory Byrne*

People who think about the past have no future.
                                        Hermione Gingold

You can only predict things after they've taken place.
                                        Eugene Ionesco

Being busy is the best excuse for not working.
                                        Kenneth Tynan

When you drop the soap in the bath, it always goes to the last place you go groping for it with your hand. This is intuitive.   *Pat Ingoldsby*

Any wire cut to exactly the length will be too short.
                                        Arthur Bloch

No matter which train you're waiting for, the wrong one always comes first.   *Miles Kington*

The worst thing about getting away from it all is that when you arrive, you usually discover somebody else has brought it all with them.   *Arnold Palmer*

Life is too short to learn German.   *Richard Porson*

The art of pleasing consists in being pleased.
William Hazlitt

I hate housework. You make the beds, you do the dishes – and six months later you have to start all over again.
Joan Rivers

LITERATURE

A writer has nothing to say after the age of forty. If he's clever enough he knows how to disguise that fact.
Georges Simenon

The best use of a book of poetry is for killing persistent flies.
Geoffrey Grigson

When you look up from your typewriter, look at the trees, not the calendar.
Mary Micka

Literature is mostly about sex and not much about children. Life is the other way round.
David Lodge

Being a writer in Hollywood gives you an opportunity to fly first class, be treated like a celebrity, sit around the pool . . . and be betrayed.
Ian McEwan

Writers should be read, but neither seen nor heard.
Daphne du Maurier

If Shelley had been a gardener he would have known that when winter comes, spring is invariably far behind.
Spike Hughes

Irish Drama Rules O'Casey.   *Graffiti*

If I had to give young writers advice, I'd say don't listen to writers talking about writing.   *Lillian Hellman*

Some editors are failed writers, but so are most writers.
T S Eliot

John Dryden's imagination resembled the wings of an ostrich: it enabled him to run, though not to soar.
Lord Macaulay

I like thin books because they balance tables, leather volumes because they can strop razors, and heavy books because they can be thrown at the cat.
Mark Twain

The three essentials for an autobiography are that its compiler should have an eccentric father, a miserable misunderstood childhood, and a hell of a time at public school.   *P G Wodehouse*

A bad review is even less important than whether it's raining in Patagonia.   *Iris Murdoch*

I read in a book that cigarettes were bad for you so I had to give up reading.   *Anon*

The secret to writing is to go through your stuff until you come on something you think is particularly good, and then cut it out.   *P G Wodehouse*

Hell hath no fury like a hustler with a literary agent.

Frank Sinatra

I read newspapers avidly. It is my one form of continuous fiction.

Aneurin Bevan

Having been unpopular in high school is not just cause for book publication.

Fran Lebowitz

I have nothing to say and I'm saying it and that is poetry.

John Cage

Advertisements contain the only truths to be relied on in a newspaper.

Thomas Jefferson

Journalists don't live by words alone, though sometimes they have to eat them.

Adlai Stevenson

A good bishop denouncing a book from the pulpit with the right organ note to his voice can add between fifteen to twenty thousand to the sales.

P G Wodehouse

There's no such thing as bad publicity except an obituary.

Brendan Behan

I never read a book before reviewing it. It prejudices a man so.

Sydney Smith

When two people are collaborating on the same book, each believes he gets all the worries and only half the royalties.

Agatha Christie

For a man to be a poet, he must be either in love or miserable.
                                        Lord Byron

One of the fallacies of summer holidays is that you're going to get some serious reading done while you're lying on the beach.
                                        Nancy Stahl

Writing would be a wonderful occupation except for the paperwork.
                                        Peter de Vries

The best impromptu speeches are the ones written well in advance.
                                        Ruth Gordon

When in doubt, ascribe all quotations to George Bernard Shaw.
                                        Nigel Rees

The possession of a book often becomes a substitute for not reading it.
                                        Anthony Burgess

Authors are easy enough to get on with, if you're fond of children.
                                        Michael Joseph

Why do people feel that writing dull books about, say, Shakespeare's humour is respectable, but writing funny books themselves is *infra dig*?
                                        P G Wodehouse

Drama never changed anybody's mind about anything.
                                        David Mamet

You can start changing the world with a biro and the back of a bus ticket.
                                        Pat Ingoldsby

Britain has made two invaluable contributions to
civilisation: the detective novel and tea.   *Ayn Rand*

It's the gossip columnist's business to write about what
is none of his business.   *Louis Kronenberger*

A good novel tells us the truth about its hero, but a
bad novel tells us the truth about its author.
G K Chesterton

I have made this letter longer than usual only because I
have not had the time to make it shorter.   *Blaise Pascal*

It is very pleasant to be written about, even by a writer.
Joyce Cary

Why don't you write books people can understand?
Nora Barnacle to her husband James Joyce

No, she was fatter than me.
Nora Barnacle after being asked if she 'was' Molly Bloom

The art of newspaper paragraphing is to stroke a
platitude until it purrs like an epigram.   *Don Marquis*

Only two classes of books are of universal appeal: the
very best and the very worst.   *Ford Madox Ford*

The best time for planning a book is when you're
doing the dishes.   *Agatha Christie*

Better to write for yourself and have no public than to
write for the public and have no self.   *Cyril Connolly*

Show me a hero and I will write a tragedy.
F Scott Fitzgerald

I read books like mad but I'm careful not to let anything I read influence me. *Michael Caine*

You will never write a good book until you have written some bad ones. *George Bernard Shaw*

Anyone who's going to be a writer knows enough at fifteen to write several novels. *May Sarton*

If all George Bernard Shaw's books were laid end to end, it would still be raining in Dublin. *Graffiti*

You need a skin as thin as a cigarette paper to write a new novel, and the hide of an elephant to publish it.
Frank Davison

There are three rules for writing the novel. Unfortunately, no one knows what they are. *W Somerset Maugham*

The reason very few people care for poetry is because very few poets care for people. *Tony Curtis*

Everybody writes a book too many. *Mordecai Richler*

Autobiographies ought to begin with Chapter Two.
Ellery Sedgwick

In journalism there are men – and women – who have doubts about Papal infallibility. But none about their own. *Con Houlihan*

An author's first duty is to let down his country.
Brendan Behan

One writer I know has the unnerving habit of making two extra copies of all his love letters – one for himself and the other for the British Museum. *Jilly Cooper*

Joyce's *Ulysses* is merely the scratching of pimples on the body of the bootboy at Claridges. *Virginia Woolf*

Virginia Woolf's writing is no more than glamorous knitting. I believe she must have a pattern somewhere.
Edith Sitwell

I prefer dead writers because you don't run into them at parties. *Fran Lebowitz*

To say that Agatha Christie's characters are cardboard cut-outs is an insult to cardboard cut-outs. *Ruth Rendell*

His sentences run from here to the airport.
Carolyn Chute on William Faulkner

Mills & Boon with wonderbras. *Kathy Lette on chicklit*

Shakespeare is so tiring. You never get a chance to sit down unless you're a king. *Josephine Hull*

Aldous Huxley is a stupid person's idea of a clever person. *Elizabeth Bowen*

I read about writers' lives with the grim fascination of someone slowing down to get a good look at a car accident.

Kaye Gibbons

It is the sexless novel that should be distinguished. The sex novel is now normal.

George Bernard Shaw

Remarks are not literature.

Gertrude Stein

Books are what they make films out of for TV.

Robert Morley

Everywhere I go I'm asked if the universities stifle writers. My opinion is that they don't stifle enough of them.

Flannery O'Connor

Writers have two main problems. One is writer's block, when the words won't come at all, and the other is logorrhoea, when the words come so fast that they can hardly get to the wastebasket on time.

Cecilia Bartholomew

The biggest critics of my books are people who never read them.

Jackie Collins

A bit of trash now and then is good for the severest reader. It provides the necessary roughage in the literary diet.

Phyllis McGinley

I read a book recently that had too many characters and no plot. When I brought it back to the library they said, 'Why did you steal the phone book?'

Dorothy Fraser

No self-respecting fish should be wrapped in a
Murdoch newspaper.   *Mike Royko*

LOVE

Women are not in love with me but with the picture
of me on the screen. I am merely the canvas on which
women paint their dreams.   *Rudolph Valentino*

Love is generally valued at its highest during two
periods in life: during the days of courting and the
days in court.   *Lee Marvin*

Friendship is a disinterested commerce between equals;
love an abject intercourse between tyrants and slaves.
                                      Oliver Goldsmith

Love is the most subtle form of self-interest.
                                      Holbrook Jackson

Because women can do nothing except love, they've
given it a ridiculous importance.   *W Somerset Maugham*

A career is a wonderful thing, but you can't snuggle up
to it on a cold night.   *Marilyn Monroe*

It's in our thirties that we want friendship. By the
forties we realise that won't save us any more than love
did.   *F Scott Fitzgerald*

Love is what you feel for a dog or a pussycat. It doesn't apply to humans.
Johnny Rotten

Love is just another four-letter word.
Tennessee Williams

When a person falls in love, he doesn't care about Biafra.
Françoise Sagan

Love is a game of secret stratagems in which only the fools who are fated to lose reveal their true motives.
Eugene O'Neill

What is love? The need to escape from oneself.
Charles Baudelaire

There's no such thing as love. Take a romantic couple to Ethiopia, where there's no food, and they'll eat each other.
Howard Stern

Self-love seems so often unrequited.
Anthony Powell

The less we love a woman, the more we are loved by her.
Alexander Pushkin

One should always be in love. That is the reason one should never marry.
Oscar Wilde

Perhaps at 14, every boy should be in love with some ideal woman to put on a pedestal and worship. As he grows up, of course, he will put her on a pedestal the better to view her legs.
Barry Norman

Love is the history of a woman's life. It is an episode in
a man's.   *Madame de Stael*

A love affair nowadays is a tableau of two wild animals,
each with its teeth sunk in the other's neck, each scared
to let go in case it bleeds to death.   *Kenneth Tynan*

In their first passions women are in love with their
lover; in all the rest, with love.   *La Rochefoucauld*

It's passion that makes the world go round. Love just
makes it a safer place.   *Ice-T*

Love is being stupid together.   *Paul Valery*

Physical love, forbidden as it was 20 or 30 years ago,
has now become boringly obligatory.   *Françoise Sagan*

By the time you say you're his
Shivering and sighing
And you swear your passion is
Infinite, undying
Lady, make a note of this
One of you is lying.   *Dorothy Parker*

Kissing may be the language of love, but money does
the talking.   *Anon*

Infatuation means a love that it is inconvenient to go
on with.   *Celia Fremlin*

The only really queer people are those who don't love anybody. *Rita Mae Brown on homosexuality*

Love makes the time pass; time makes love pass. *Anon*

Of all forms of caution, caution in love is perhaps the most fatal to true happiness. *Bertrand Russell*

Love is like photography – it develops in the dark.
Noel Coward

It's easier to love humanity as a whole than to love one's neighbour. *Eric Hoffer*

A man falls in love through his eyes, a woman through her ears. *Woodrow Wyatt*

In real love you want the other person's good. In romantic love you want the other person.
Margaret Anderson

I here and now, finally and forever, give up knowing anything about love, or wanting to know. I believe it doesn't exist, save as a word. It's a sort of wailing phoenix that is really the wind in the trees.
D H Lawrence

Love is the delightful interval between meeting a beautiful girl and deciding she looks like a haddock.
John Barrymore

A woman does not want her love affairs talked about.
Yet she wants everyone to know that someone loves her.
André Maurois

One can find women who have never had one love
affair . . . but it is rare indeed to find any who have
had *only* one.
La Rochefoucauld

Love does not consist in gazing at one another, but in
looking together in the same direction.
Antoine de Saint-Exupéry

Love isn't the dying moan of a distant violin – it's the
triumphant twang of a bedspring.
S J Perelman

Some of the greatest love affairs I've ever known
involved one actor, unassisted.
Wilson Mizner

It is the nature of women not to love when we love
them, and to love when we love them not.
Cervantes

Much of what we call love is in fact mutually indulged
laziness.
Kenneth Tynan

All discarded lovers should be given a second chance –
but with somebody else.
Mae West

There is no fury like an ex-wife searching for a new
lover.
Cyril Connolly

I love you no matter what you do – but do you have
to do so much of it?
Jean Illsley Clarke

No one has ever loved anyone the way everyone wants to be loved.
Mignon McLaughlin

I love Mickey Mouse more than any woman I've ever known.
Walt Disney

I don't want to live. I want to love first, and live incidentally.
Zelda Fitzgerald

Face it: love isn't like the movies. Walt Disney and Doris Day lied to us. I want my money back.
Jean Mitchell

I never liked the men I loved and I never loved the men I liked.
Fanny Brice

When you're in love with someone you want to be near him all the time, except when you're out buying things and charging them to him.
Miss Piggy

Much more genius is needed to make love than to command armies.
Ninon de Lenclos

Love your enemy – it will drive him nuts.   *Eleanor Doan*

To be happy with a man you must understand him a lot and love him a little. To be happy with a woman you must love her a lot and not try to understand her at all.
Helen Rowland

Love is only a dirty trick played on us to achieve the continuation of the species.   *W Somerset Maugham*

A woman has got to love a bad man once or twice in her life to be thankful for a good one.   *Marjorie Rawlings*

Love is moral without legal marriage, but marriage is immoral without love.   *Ellen Kay*

I live my whole life around my man – work, play, dreams, everything. When I am alone I am lost. I can only find myself with a lover. Some actors say they can only exist when they are playing a role. Me, I can only play a role, only exist, when I am loved.   *Brigitte Bardot*

There are very few people who are not ashamed of having been in love when they no longer love each other.   *La Rochefoucauld*

I doubt whether any girl would be satisfied with her lover's mind if she knew the whole of it.   *Anthony Trollope*

Love is like a cigar. If it goes out, you can light it again – but it never tastes quite the same.   *Lord Wavell*

Cruelty, possessiveness and petty jealousy are traits you develop when in love.   *Noel Coward*

A lover without indiscretion is no lover at all.   *Thomas Hardy*

Love is like the measles – all the worse when it comes late in life.   *Douglas Jerrold*

Better to have loved and lost than to have paid for it and not enjoyed it.
Graffiti

Better to have loved and lost than loved and married.
Sammy Shore

Love is a disease which fills you with a desire to be desired.
Henri, Comte de Toulouse Lautrec

Love is what's left over after *being* in love has burned away.
Louis de Bernières

What better proof can there be of love than money?
Quentin Crisp

Love is a fan club with only two fans.
Adrian Henri

I can understand companionship. I can understand bought sex in the afternoon. I cannot understand the love affair.
Gore Vidal

Love built on beauty, soon as beauty, dies.
John Donne

I loved my mother from the day she died.
Michael Hartnett

I believe the nearest I have come to perfect love was with a young coal-miner when I was about 16.
D H Lawrence

Scratch a lover and find a foe.
Dorothy Parker

Love cures everything except poverty and toothache.
Mae West

We have to realise that we are as deeply afraid to live and to love as we are to die. *R D Laing*

It is very rarely that a man loves. And when he does, it is nearly always fatal. *Hugh McDiarmid*

Love has been defined as 'The cognitive-affective state characterised by intrusive and obsessive fantasising concerning reciprocity of amorant feelings by the object of the amorance'. *Richard Wilson*

Broken hearts die slowly. *Thomas Campbell*

To love another is to see oneself as an other to the other. *R D Laing*

Let no one who loves be called altogether unhappy. Even love unreturned has its rainbow. *J M Barrie*

To a woman who deeply loves a man, broken betrothal is as death itself. Indeed, it is worse. *Marie Stopes*

I was counting my Valentine cards. This didn't take long, as I had exactly none. *Rhona Cameron*

Follow love and it will flee.
Flee it, and it follows ye. *Proverb*

Love is knowing how to join the temperament of a vampire with the discretion of an anemone.   *E M Cioran*

A man can be happy with any woman as long as he does not love her.
                                                    Oscar Wilde

Love is so much better when you're not married.
                                                    Maria Callas

Nothing is better for the spirit than a love affair. It elevates thought and flattens stomachs.   *Barbara Howar*

I knew I was falling in love with her because I read it every day in the newspapers.
            Eddie Fisher in wry mood about his courtship of Debbie Reynolds

Greater love than this no man hath, that a man lay down his wife for his friend.   *James Joyce*

Love is like quicksilver in the hand. Leave the fingers open and it stays; clutch it and it darts away.
                                                    Dorothy Parker

MARRIAGE

I feel sure that no girl would go to the altar if she knew all.   *Queen Victoria*

One doesn't have to get anywhere in a marriage. It's not a public conveyance.   *Iris Murdoch*

Love means never having to say you're sorry. Marriage is never having a chance to say *anything*.   **Hal Roach**

The first part of our marriage was happy. But then, on the way out of the church . . .   **Henny Youngman**

The ultimate penalty for bigamy is two mothers-in-law.   **George Russell**

To get the American divorce rate, get the marriage rate and divide by one.   **Zero Mostel**

I belong to Bridegrooms Anonymous. Whenever I feel like getting married, they send over a lady in a housecoat and curlers to scream at me and burn the toast.   **Dick Martin**

There are two sides to every argument. And they're usually married to one another.   **George Burns**

Many a man owes his success to his first wife, and his second wife to his success.   **Jim Backus**

Any husband who buys wallpaper, drapes or even a living-room rug on his own is auditioning for the Bureau of Missing Persons.   **Bill Crosby**

When a man marries his mistress, he creates a job opportunity.   **Sir James Goldsmith**

I've sometimes thought of murder, but never divorce.   **Charlton Heston**

The occasional lacing of my husband's dinner with cat food has done wonders for my spirit. *Lana Tate*

Marriage is a wonderful invention. But then again, so is the bicycle repair kit. *Billy Connolly*

The dread of loneliness is greater than the fear of bondage, so we get married. *Cyril Connolly*

Most marriages don't add two people together. They subtract one from the other. *Ian Fleming*

Marriage requires a special talent, like acting. And monogamy requires *genius*. *Warren Beatty*

A bachelor has the right idea about marriage. He knows it's a device of society designed to make trouble between two people who would otherwise get along very well. *Anthony Quinn*

A husband should not insult his wife publicly at parties. He should wait until he gets back to the privacy of the home to do so. *James Thurber*

All men make mistakes, but those who are married find out about them sooner. *Red Skelton*

George Bush reminds every woman of her first husband. *Jane O'Reilly*

I can trust my husband not to fall asleep on a public platform – and he usually claps in the right place.

Margaret Thatcher

Second marriages collapse at twice the rate of first ones.

Maggie Drummond

If your husband has difficulty getting to sleep, the words 'We need to talk about our relationship' should help.

Rita Rudner

When I got divorced I went through the various stages of grieving: anger, denial, dancing round my settlement cheque . . .

Maura Kennedy

Many a wife thinks her husband is the world's greatest lover; she just can't catch him at it.

Mamie van Doren

When you're single again, at the beginning you're very optimistic and you say, 'I want to meet someone who's really smart, really sweet, really sensitive'. Then six months later you're like, 'Lord, any mammal with a day job'.

Carol Liefer

Divorce is an institution only a few weeks later in origin than marriage.

Voltaire

Why marry a ball-player when you can have the whole team?

Mae West on Marilyn Monroe's marriage to baseball player Joe di Maggio

Never marry an actress on account of they have their careers and work bad hours. *Ernest Hemingway*

Every woman is entitled to a middle husband she can forget. *Adela Rogers St John*

If you're afraid of loneliness, don't marry. *Anton Chekhov*

When you're bored with yourself, marry and be bored with someone else. *David Pryce-Jones*

Before marriage she talks and he listens. After marriage he talks and she listens. After a few years nobody talks and the neighbours listen. *Henny Youngman*

Divorce is when you don't bring home the bacon any more – you just post it. *Morty Craft*

These days an old-fashioned marriage is one that outlasts the wedding gifts. *Hal Roach*

Nothing ages a man quite like living always with the same woman. *Norman Douglas*

Whenever a husband and wife begin to discuss their marriage, they are giving evidence at an inquest. *Elbert Hubbard*

I've been in love with the same woman for 41 years. If my wife finds out, she'll kill me. *Henny Youngman*

Ninety per cent of ulcers are married ones. They come from mortgages, commuter rides, yard work, flooded basements and fighting over who leaves the toilet lid up and why she calls the bar to see if he left yet.

Mike Royko

I knew Elizabeth Taylor when she didn't know where her next husband was coming from.   *Johnny Carson*

My wife has an impediment in her speech. Every now and then she stops to take a breath.

Kevin Goldstein-Jackson

The majority of husbands remind me of an orang-utan trying to play the violin.   *Honoré de Balzac*

I used to live alone. Then I got divorced.   *Bob Hoskins*

He tricked me into marrying him. He told me I was pregnant.   *Carol Liefer*

The difference between an Irish wedding and an Irish wake is . . . one less drunk.   *Niall Toibin*

By all means marry. If you get a good wife you'll be happy. If you don't, you'll become a philosopher.

Socrates

Some people ask the secret of the long marriage of myself and my wife. It's like this. We both go to a restaurant twice a week. A little candlelight, dinner, soft music and dancing. She goes Thursdays, I go Fridays.   *Henny Youngman*

'Tis safest in matrimony to begin with a little aversion.
R B Sheridan

Don't trust your horse in the field, or your wife in the house.
Leo Tolstoy

A man who boasts he never made a mistake married a woman who did.
Herbert Prochnow

Husbands are like fires. They go out when unattended.
Zsa Zsa Gabor

Never feel remorse for what you've thought about your wife, for she's thought much worse things about you.
Jean Rostand

The most difficult year in marriage is the one you're in.
Franklin P Jones

Divorce is excruciating. It's like mourning a death, only worse – because the damn corpse keeps waking up.
Erica Jong

He married a woman to stop her getting away. Now she's there all day.
Philip Larkin

There's so little difference between husbands, you might as well keep the first one.
Adela Rogers St John

Niagara Falls is only the second biggest disappointment of the standard honeymoon.
Oscar Wilde

The best part of marriage is the fights. The rest is merely so-so.
Thornton Wilder

The honeymoon is over when he phones to say he'll be late for supper, and she's already left a note to say it's in the fridge.
Bill Lawrence

My mother-in-law broke up my marriage. One day my wife came home and found us in bed together.
Lenny Bruce

It's only possible to live happily ever after on a day-to-day basis.
Margaret Bonnano

The trouble with most lovers is that they have a habit of turning into husbands.
Diana Dors

A young man married is a young man that's marred.
William Shakespeare

Many a man in love with a dimple makes the mistake of marrying the whole girl.
Stephen Leacock

American marriages operate on the premise of 'Till debt do us part'.
Johnny Carson

Husbands rarely understand their wives. Wives understand their husbands all too well.
John Train

An old man marrying a young girl is like buying a book for someone else to read.
H W Thompson

You can't expect to take your wife shopping and just come out with what you went in for.   *J B Boothroyd*

My mother was desperate to get me married. She used to say, 'Sure he's a murderer. But a *single* murderer.'
Joan Rivers

No one should marry until he has studied anatomy and dissected at least one woman.   *Honoré de Balzac*

Killing your wife is a natural thing that could happen to the best of us.   *Brendan Behan*

I was married by a judge. I should have asked for a jury.   *Sylvester Stallone*

A little compatibility in marriage is always to be advised – provided the man has the income and the woman is pattable.   *Nathan Quigley*

When a girl marries, she exchanges the attentions of many men for the inattentions of one.   *Helen Rowland*

Many a wife has discovered that hugging her husband is the best way to get around him.   *James Simpson*

Liz Taylor's philosophy of marriage is: Always the bride, never the bridesmaid.   *Joan Rivers*

By persistently remaining single, a man converts himself into a permanent public temptation.
Oscar Wilde

Let's be honest: a wedding is absolutely the worst way to start married life. *Caitlin Moran*

The best thing about living on a farm is that you can fight with your wife without being heard. *Kin Hubbard*

A man is incomplete until he's married. Then he's finished. *Zsa Zsa Gabor*

Don't worry about Alan; he'll always land on somebody's feet. *Dorothy Parker of her husband*

Keep your eyes wide open before marriage, and half shut afterwards. *Benjamin Franklin*

When a man brings flowers home to his wife for no reason, there's a reason. *James Simpson*

People don't realise what happiness is until they get married – and by then it's too late. *Artie Shaw*

The proper basis for marriage is a mutual misunderstanding. *Oscar Levant*

Marriage is all right, but it's carrying love a bit far. *Texas Guinan*

Marriage is only for a little while. It's alimony that lasts forever. *Quentin Crisp*

Bachelors should be heavily taxed. It is not fair that some men should be happier than others. *Oscar Wilde*

There's a woman for every man in the world. And he's damn lucky if his wife doesn't find out about her.

Mort Sahl

There are only about 20 murders a year in Britain and not all are serious. Some are just husbands killing their wives.

G H Hatherill

A woman should have a prosaic husband and a romantic lover.

Stendhal

When divorces become so cheap that the poor can afford them, the last social distinction will be gone.

Herbert Prochnow

People sometimes commit bigamy for no better reason than to please the landlady.

Gerald Dodson

Marriage is a lot like the army. Everyone complains, but you'd be surprised at how many re-enlist.

James Garner

Never trust a husband too far – or a bachelor too near.

Helen Rowland

Bigamy is having one wife too many. Monogamy is the same thing.

Oscar Wilde

A bride's attitude towards her betrothed can be summed up in three words: Aisle Altar Hymn.

Frank Muir

Marriage is the process whereby a woman tries to turn a man from an old rake into a lawnmower.   *Hal Roach*

The only thing that holds most marriages together is the husband being big enough to stand back and see where his wife went wrong.   *Archie Bunker*

Being an old maid is like death by drowning: a delightful sensation after you cease to struggle.
Edna Ferber

Marriage is give and take. You'd better give it or she'll take it anyway.   *Joey Adams*

If you want to read a book about love and marriage, you've got to read two separate books.   *Alan King*

Love is the quest, marriage the conquest and divorce the inquest.   *Helen Rowland*

An otherwise happily married couple may turn a mixed doubles game [of tennis] into a scene from *Who's Afraid of Virginia Woolf.*   *Rod Laver*

I've married a few people I shouldn't have, but then haven't we all?   *Mamie van Doren*

Some of us are becoming the men we wanted to marry.
Gloria Steinem

Monotony is only having one wife.   *Don Rickles*

All men are born free, but some of them get married.

Simon Grey

A bachelor never Mrs anyone.

Dave Allen

If wives were good, God would have had one.

Proverb

Divorce costs more than marriage but it's worth it.

Johnny Carson

Marriage isn't a word; it's a sentence.

Henny Youngman

A man marries to have a home, but also because he doesn't want to be bothered by sex and all that sort of thing.

W Somerset Maugham

Marriage should be grounds for divorce.

Mickey Rooney

One can always recognise women who trust their husbands. They look so thoroughly unhappy.

Oscar Wilde

A man would often be the lover of his wife if he were married to someone else.

Elinor Glyn

Being divorced is like being hit by a Mack truck. If you live through it, you start looking very carefully to the right and left.

Jean Kerr

Getting divorced because you don't love a man is about as silly as getting married just because you *do*.

Zsa Zsa Gabor

I'd rather be a beggar and single than a Queen and married.
Queen Elizabeth I

The only really happy people are married women and single men.
Marlene Dietrich

My wife got the house, the car, the bank account, and if I marry again and have children, she gets them too.
Woody Allen

It's difficult to tell which gives females the most happiness – the minister who marries or the judge who divorces.
Mary Little

When you see what some girls marry, you realise how much they must hate to work for a living.
Helen Rowland

The secret of a successful marriage is not to be at home too much.
Colin Chapman

In my day, men were content with ten commandments and one wife. Now the situation is reversed.
Saki

A man with a career can have no time to waste upon his wife and friends; he has to devote it wholly to his enemies.
John Oliver Hobbes

Women who remember their first kiss now have daughters who can't remember their first husbands.
Henny Youngman

I shall marry in haste, and repeat at leisure.
James Branch Cabell

My best friend ran away with my wife, and let me tell you – I miss him.
Henny Youngman

Next to privacy, the rarest thing in Hollywood is a wedding anniversary.
Gene Fowler

My wife says I never listen to her. At least that's what I *think* she said.
Milton Berle

Divorce happens when you haven't been home for 18 years.
Lee Trevino

In marriage, a man becomes slack and selfish, and undergoes a fatty degeneration of his moral being.
Robert Louis Stevenson

Marriage interferes with romance. Any time you have a romance, your wife is bound to interfere.
Groucho Marx

When I was with Elizabeth Taylor I knew what was missing in my marriage to Debbie Reynolds. Everything.
Eddie Fisher

The honeymoon wasn't such a ghastly experience really. It was afterwards that was so awful.
Noel Coward

The Vietnam War finally ended in an agreement neither side ever intended to honour. It was like one of Zsa Zsa Gabor's weddings.
Bob Hope

Marilyn Monroe's marriage to Joe DiMaggio didn't work out because he found out she wasn't Marilyn Monroe. Her marriage to Arthur Miller didn't work out because he found out she was.   *Billy Wilder*

It was a Scottish wedding – the confetti was on elastic.
      Bob Monkhouse

Marriage is like pleading guilty to a crime you can't remember committing, and being sentenced to life imprisonment . . . without parole.   *Artie Shaw*

Henry VIII didn't get divorced. He had his wives' heads chopped off when he got tired with them. That's a good way to get rid of a woman. No alimony.
      Ted Turner

Marriage is the best magician there is. In front of your eyes it can change a cute little dish into a boring dishwasher.   *Jerry Lewis*

There are two times in a woman's life when she doesn't understand men: (i) before marriage, and (ii) after marriage.   *Jean Kerr*

Marriage is the process of discovering what type of man your wife would have preferred.   *Hal Roach*

It is easier to be a lover than a husband for the same reason it is more difficult to show a ready wit all day long than to produce an occasional *bon mot*.
      Honoré de Balzac

The reason that husbands and wives don't understand one another is because they belong to different sexes.

Dorothy Dix

The main problem with marriage is that men won't act their ages and women won't tell theirs.   **Bob Hope**

My wife said, 'Can my mother come down for the weekend?' I said, 'Why?' She said, 'Two weeks is far too long to leave anyone on the roof.'   **Bob Monkhouse**

A man's friend likes him but leaves him as he is: his wife loves him and is always trying to turn him into somebody else.   **G K Chesterton**

My husband said he needed more space, so I locked him outside.   **Roseanne**

I married beneath me. All women do.   **Nancy Astor**

In a two-car family, the wife always has the smaller car.

Ruth Rendell

Wives are like cockroaches. They'll survive after a nuclear attack.   **Lorrie Moore**

I went into marriage with both eyes closed. Her father closed one and her brother closed the other.

Max Kauffmann

Marriage is lonelier than solitude.   **Beverley Sills**

If there's one thing better than marrying a millionaire, it's divorcing him. *Zsa Zsa Gabor*

At every party there are two kinds of people – those who want to go and those who don't. Unfortunately, they're usually married to each other. *Ann Landers*

The wages of sin is alimony. *Carolyn Wells*

Men rarely dream about getting married. Women have a magazine called *Bride*, but there's no magazine called *Groom*. *Mary Reinholz*

Any woman who thinks marriage is a fifty-fifty proposition either doesn't understand men or percentages. *Florynce Kennedy*

Never marry a man who hates his mother – because he'll end up hating you. *Jill Bennett*

Nothing happened in our marriage. I nicknamed the water bed Lake Placid. *Phyllis Diller*

The best way to solve the problems between the sexes would be to make marriage very difficult and divorce very easy, instead of the reverse. *Glenda Jackson*

The best way to get revenge on a man you hate is to marry him. *Ava Gardner*

If you have a female child, set her to sewing and not reading. Teach her to be useful in the house – to make bread, to clean chickens, to sift, cook, launder and spin, to put new feet into socks, and so on. Then, when you marry her off, she won't seem an ignoramus.

Paolo de Certaldo

A wise woman will always let her husband have her way.

R B Sheridan

My wife is on a diet of coconuts and bananas. She hasn't lost any weight, but she can sure climb a tree.

Henny Youngman

Most men flirt with the women they would not marry and marry the women who would not flirt with them.

Ian Fleming

In Hollywood, men get married in the morning. That way, if it doesn't work out, you haven't wasted a whole day.

Mickey Rooney

Every man is thoroughly happy twice in his life: just after he has met his first love, and just after he has left his last one.

H L Mencken

Marry an outdoor woman. Then if you throw her out in the yard for the night, she can still survive.

W C Fields

Husbands are chiefly good as lovers when they are betraying their wives.

Marilyn Monroe

Basically my wife was immature. I'd be at home in my bath and she'd come in and sink my boats.   *Woody Allen*

I didn't marry my wife because she had £4 million. I would have married her if she only had £2 million.
Charles Forte

I bequeathed my entire estate to my wife on condition that she married again. I want to be sure that there will be at least one other man who will regret my death.
Heinrich Heine

It's too bad that in most marriage ceremonies they don't use the word 'obey' any more. It used to lend a little humour to the occasion.   *Lloyd Cory*

If you're married, it only takes one to make a quarrel.
Ogden Nash

I can't for the life of me understand why people keep insisting that marriage is doomed. All five of mine worked out.   *Peter de Vries*

I didn't want to marry her; she didn't want to marry me. It was obvious we were meant for each other.
Eddie Fisher on his relationship with Connie Stevens

The first thrill of adultery is entering the house. Everything has been paid for by the other man.
John Updike

Men who don't understand women fall into two categories: bachelors and husbands.   *Jacques Languirand*

I knew a guy who had a heart attack, so he got a pacemaker. His wife divorced him because she said it interfered with the TV. **Walter Matthau**

I have certainly known more men destroyed by the desire to have a wife and child and to keep them in comfort than I have seen destroyed by drink and harlots. **William Butler Yeats**

How marriage ruins a man. It's as demoralising as cigarettes . . . and far more expensive. **Oscar Wilde**

One year I bought the wife a fireside chair. It cost me a lot of money. That's why I was annoyed that it fused when I plugged it in. **Les Dawson**

Marriage is a ghastly public confession of a strictly private intent. **Ian Hay**

A man should be taller, older, heavier, uglier and hoarser than his wife. **Edgar Howe**

No, more like a jury.
Kenneth Tynan after being asked by Cyril Connolly if his first wife was a trial

Did you hear about the new 'divorced' Barbie doll? It comes with all of Ken's stuff. **Sid Caesar**

A society in which women are taught anything but the management of a family, the care of men and the creation of the future generation is a society on the way out.
Ron Hubbard

Gentleman requires first class accommodation, full board in quiet guesthouse in seaside resort, where he can put up with his wife for the first two weeks in August.
Advertisement quoted by Patrick Myler

I got fed up being turned down by birds in the pub.
Eric Clapton on why he got married in 1979

For a while, my wife and I pondered whether to take a vacation or get a divorce. We decided that a trip to Bermuda is over in two weeks, but a divorce is something you always have.
Woody Allen

I don't worry about terrorism. I was married for two years.
Sam Kinison

A woman seldom asks advice before she has bought her wedding clothes.
Joseph Addison

Some women get even with their husbands by staying married to them.
Milton Berle

Marriage is like a dull meal with the dessert at the beginning.
Henri de Toulouse-Lautrec

There were no last words. His wife was with him to the end.
Spike Milligan

I've just got rid of ten pounds of ugly fat – I divorced the wife.
Roy 'Chubby' Brown

The next time I get married I'm going to cut out the middle man. I'll just give the house to someone I hate.
P J O'Rourke

The desire to get married is a basic and primal instinct in women. It's followed by another basic and primal instinct: the desire to be single again.
Nora Ephron

You have only to mumble a few words in church to get married, and a few words in your sleep to get divorced.
Hal Roach

Mixed emotion is watching your mother-in-law drive over a cliff in your new Ferrari.
Long John Lebel

For most ballplayers, all getting married means is that now they have to hide their datebooks.
Don Kowet

I will never marry again, never. Being married means making excuses, and I'm not a good liar. To lie you have to have a good memory, and I can't remember anything I've done for years.
Richard Harris

I wanted to marry her ever since I saw the moonlight shining on the barrel of her father's shotgun.
Eddie Albert

You may marry the man of your dreams, but fourteen years later you're living with a couch that burps.
Roseanne

I've never been married but I tell people I'm divorced so they won't think something's wrong with me.

Elayne Boosler

My husband will never chase another woman. He's too fine, too decent . . . too old. **Gracie Allen**

I love being married. It's great to find that one special person you want to annoy for the rest of your life.

Rita Rudner

Love means never having to say you're sorry. Marriage means having to say everything twice. **Estelle Getty**

I've had diseases that lasted longer than my marriages.

Nell Carter

Judging by the divorce rate, a lot of people who say 'I do' don't. **Hal Roach**

MEN & WOMEN

The Queen is most anxious to enlist everyone in checking this mad, wicked folly of 'Women's Rights'. It is a subject which makes the Queen so furious that she cannot contain herself. **Queen Victoria**

Behind almost every woman you ever heard of stands a man who let her down. **Naomi Bliven**

Love may make the world go round, but it's spinsters who oil the wheels.
Ellen Dorothy

A woman despises a man for loving her unless she returns his love.
Elizabeth Stoddard

A man likes his wife to be just clever enough to comprehend his cleverness, and just stupid enough to admire it.
Israel Zangwill

Every artist is an unhappy lover.
Iris Murdoch

If men knew how women pass their time when they're alone, they'd never marry.
O Henry

There is always one who kisses and one who allows the kiss.
George Bernard Shaw

Women must come off the pedestal. Men only put us up there to get us out of the way.
Lady Rhondo

Can you imagine a world without men? There'd be no crime, and lots of fat happy women.
Nicole Hollander

If diamonds are a girl's best friend and man's best friend is a dog, what chance do man-woman relationships have?
Cynthia Heimel

Always carry a book on a date so that when you get bored you can slip into the Ladies for a read.
Sharon Stone

Employees make the best dates. You don't have to pick them up, and they're tax deductible.   *Andy Warhol*

There's nothing so similar as one poodle dog to another and that goes for women too.   *Pablo Picasso*

A kiss can be a comma, a question mark or an exclamation point. That's basic spelling that every woman ought to know.   *Mistinguett*

The only thing a man finds harder to resist than a woman's wiles are her wails.   *Imogene Fay*

You lie to two people in your life: your girlfriend and the police. Tell the truth to everyone else.

Jack Nicholson

Constant togetherness is fine, but only for Siamese twins.   *Victoria Billings*

I like men who are prematurely wealthy.   *Joan Rivers*

Women of today – you know what they're like. 'Hi, I just had a baby an hour ago and I'm back at work already. And while I was delivering I took a seminar on tax shelter options.'   *Carol Liefer*

You never see a man walking down the street with a woman who has a little pot belly and a bald spot.

Elayne Boosler

The only men who are too young are the ones who write their love letters in crayon, wear pyjamas with feet, or fly half fare.   *Phyllis Diller*

Television has proved that people will do anything rather than look at each other.   *Ann Landers*

There's a great woman behind every idiot.   *John Lennon*

Women have a right to work wherever and whenever they please, as long as they have the dinner ready when you get home.   *John Wayne*

You can't be happy with a woman who pronounces the first 'd' in Wednesday.   *Peter de Vries*

Adam was the first eavesdropper.   *James Simpson*

Women and elephants never forget an injury.   *Saki*

You don't know a woman until you've had a letter from her.   *Ada Leverson*

A lot of post-feminist thinkers seem to have burned their brains as well as their bras.   *Kathy Lette*

Men play the game, but women know the score.   *Roger Woods*

Everyone says looks don't matter, but I never met a girl yet who fell for an ugly old guy who was broke.   *Rodney Dangerfield*

I hate feminists. They've emasculated all the men.
Carolyn Cassady

Adam should have died with all his ribs. *Graffiti*

There is more difference within the sexes than between them. *Ivy Compton-Burnett*

Men don't go shopping unless they need something.
Rita Rudner

Women sometimes forgive those who force an opportunity, never those who miss one. *Talleyrand*

A woman isn't complete without a man, but where do you find a man – I mean a real man – these days?
Lauren Bacall

It's bad manners to begin courting a widow before she comes home from the funeral. *Seamus McManus*

Women want mediocre men, and men are working to be as mediocre as possible. *Margaret Mead*

Women are cleverer than men. Did you ever see a woman marrying a man because he had lovely legs?
Bette Davis

Every little girl knows about love. It's only her capacity to suffer on account of it that increases. *Françoise Sagan*

By the time he says 'We were made for each other' he's already planning alterations. *Dorothy Parker*

The main difference between men and women is that men are lunatics and women are idiots.   *Rebecca West*

If a man opens a car door for a woman, it's either a new car or a new woman.   *Hal Roach*

Once a woman has given you her heart, you can never get rid of the rest of her.   *John Vanbrugh*

To find out a girl's faults, praise her to her girlfriends.
Benjamin Franklin

Men treat all women as sequels.   *Hal Roach*

Dancing is a wonderful training for girls. It's the first way they learn to guess what a man is going to do before he does it.   *Christopher Morley*

The cruellest revenge of a woman is to remain faithful to her man.   *Jacques Bossuet*

Certain women should be struck regularly, like gongs.
Noel Coward

If men knew what women think, they would be twenty times more audacious.   *Alphonse Karr*

The best way to turn a woman's head is to tell her she has a beautiful profile.   *Sacha Guitry*

If men could get pregnant, abortion would be a sacrament.   *Florynce Kennedy*

Courtship is when two lovers try each other for sighs.
Graffiti

Everybody winds up kissing the wrong girl goodnight.
Andy Warhol

Ian Fleming got off with women because he couldn't get on with them.
Rosamund Lehmann

Men were brought up to command, women to seduce.
Sally Kempton

The only place men want depth in a woman is in her décolletage.
Zsa Zsa Gabor

Beware of a man who praises women's liberation; he is about to quit his job.
Erica Jong

The easiest kind of relationship for me is with ten thousand people. The hardest is with one.
Janis Joplin

Men kick friendship round like a football and it doesn't seem to crack. Women treat it like glass and it goes to pieces.
Anon

A man is as good as he has to be, and a woman as bad as she dares.
Elbert Hubbard

The only thing women have got out of feminism is the privilege of going dutch.
Nora Ephron

Love affairs start when you sink in his arms – and end with your arms in his sink.
Lucille Ball

There are times when even a dedicated feminist needs a chauvinist to lean on.
Clive Cussler

A man in the house is worth two in the street.
Mae West

The man who gets on best with women is the man who knows best how to get on without them.
Charles Baudelaire

Two things a real man likes are danger and play. He likes women because they're the most dangerous playthings.
Friedrich Nietzsche

Most women will forgive a liberty easier than a slight.
Charles Colton

The hardest task in a woman's life is trying to convince a man that his intentions are honourable.
Helen Rowland

The great trick with a woman is to get rid of her while she thinks she is getting rid of you.
Soren Kierkegaard

I require only three things of a man: that he be handsome, ruthless and stupid.
Dorothy Parker

Women who love the same man have a kind of bitter freemasonry.
Max Beerbohm

When women go wrong, men go right after them.
Mae West

Even the wisest men make fools of themselves over women, and even the most foolish women are wise about men.
Theodore Reik

Love begins with a prince kissing an angel. It ends with a bald-headed man looking across the table at a fat woman.
Rodney Dangerfield

Only one man in a thousand is a leader of men. The other 999 follow women.
Groucho Marx

No woman should know more than a man if she wants to be loved.
Virginia Graham

Never despise what it says in women's magazines. It may not be subtle, but neither are men.
Zsa Zsa Gabor

When you're courting a nice girl an hour seems like a second. When you sit on a red-hot cinder, a second seems like an hour. That's relativity.
Albert Einstein

If she looks old, she's old. If she looks young, she's young. If she looks back, follow her.
Bob Hope

The only way to behave to a woman is to make love to her if she is pretty, and to someone else if she is plain.
Oscar Wilde

Give a woman an inch – and she'll park a car on it.
E B White

In point of morals, the average woman is, even for business, too crooked.
Stephen Leacock

No matter how happily a woman may be married, it always pleases her to discover that there is a nice man who wishes she were not.
H L Mencken

Next to the wound, what women make best is the bandage.
Jules Barbey d'Aurevilly

If you want anything said, ask a man. If you want something done, ask a woman.
Margaret Thatcher

A woman's desire for revenge outlasts all her other emotions.
Cyril Connolly

Behind every famous man is a woman who says there is a woman behind every famous man.
Hal Roach

Thirty-five is a very attractive age. London society is full of women of the very highest birth who have, of their own free choice, remained thirty-five for years.
Oscar Wilde

Women do not find it difficult nowadays to behave like men, but they often find it extremely difficult to behave like gentlemen.
Compton MacKenzie

That, my Lord, depends on whether I embrace your mistress or your principles.
John Wilkes after being told by Lord Sandwich that he would either die of the pox or on the gallows

Feminism is the result of a few ignorant and literal-minded women letting the cat out of the bag about which is the superior sex. **P J O'Rourke**

Friendship among women is only a suspension of hostilities. **Mort Sahl**

A feminist is a woman, usually ill-favoured, in whom the film-making instinct has replaced the maternal one.
Barry Humphries

Women aren't much, but they're the best other sex we have. **Don Herold**

Give a man a free hand and he'll run it all over you.
Mae West

A smart girl is one who knows how to play tennis, golf, piano . . . and dumb. **Marilyn Monroe**

The main reason guys will never admit to having even the teeniest clue about what women really want is because, if they did, they'd have to do something about it. **Barbara Graham**

If my husband ever met a woman who looked like the ones in his paintings, he would fall over in a dead faint.
Picasso's wife

There aren't enough men to go around. Every time there's a plane crash and I hear 100 men have been killed, I think, 'Why couldn't some women have been on that flight?'   *Helen Gurley Brown*

Anniversaries are like toilets. Men usually manage to miss them.   *Jo Brand*

A kiss that speaks volumes is rarely a first edition.
                                    Clare Whiting

When I was informed that women would be ruling the world in the year 2100 I replied, 'You mean still?'
                                    Winston Churchill

Don't ever hate a man too much to give him his diamonds back.   *Zsa Zsa Gabor*

She wore far too much rouge last night and not quite enough clothes. That is always a sign of despair in a woman.   *Oscar Wilde*

Girls are dynamite. If you don't believe that, try dropping one.   *Hal Roach*

A girl never pursues a man – but then a mousetrap never pursues a mouse.   *Ronnie Barker*

The Sunday papers are the same every week – those ghastly obligatory articles by women on how awful it is to be a woman.   *Jeffrey Bernard*

The first conjuring trick was the production of a woman from a man's rib, but it was not very well rehearsed.   *Lambert Jeffries*

I do not spoil women. I am not what is known as 'attentive'. I do not send flowers or gifts. I do none of these things because I have found it isn't necessary. I'm saving all that for when I am an old man and have to.
                    George Sanders

A woman's mind is cleaner than a man's – that's because she changes it more often.   *Oliver Hereford*

Nowadays a man can't step up and kill a woman without feeling a bit unchivalrous about it.
                    Robert Benchley

Somewhere on this earth, every ten seconds, a woman gives birth to a child. We must find this woman and stop her at once.   *Sam Levenson*

A whole generation of females wanted to ride off into a sandy Paradise with Rudolph Valentino. At thirteen I had been such a female.   *Bette Davis*

Women have served all these centuries as looking-glasses, possessing the magic and delicious power of reflecting the figure of man at twice its normal size.   *Virginia Woolf*

I don't wish women to have power over men – but over themselves.   *Simone de Beauvoir*

It is hard to fight the enemy who has outposts in your head.
Sally Kempton

My fiancé and I are having a little disagreement. What I want is a big church wedding with bridesmaids and flowers and a no-expense spared reception. What he wants is to break off our engagement.
Sally Poplin

I really like being single. Except for the bit about not having a man.
Jane Christie

Plain women know more about men than beautiful ones do.
Katharine Hepburn

I always meet men who don't want to get involved. I dated my last boyfriend for two years before finally giving him an ultimatum. 'Either you tell me your name or it's over,' I said.
Rita Rudner

All this fuss about sleeping together! For physical pleasure I'd sooner go to my dentist any day.
Evelyn Waugh

My grandmother's 90. She's dating. He's 93. They never argue. They can't hear each other.
Cathy Ladman

A curved line is the loveliest distance between two points.
Mae West

Men seldom make passes at girls who wear glasses.
Dorothy Parker

Men look *at* themselves in mirrors; women look *for* themselves.
Elissa Melamed

It is really a very hard life. Men will not be nice to you if you are not good-looking, and women will not be nice to you if you are.
Agatha Christie

When a man of sixty runs off with a young woman, I'm never surprised. I have a sneaking admiration for him. I wish him luck. After all, he's going to need it.
Deborah Kerr

A woman's place is in the kitchen and the bedroom and taking care of her kids. You find one that's happy – she won't be out looking for a job.
Evel Knievel

The desirable things in life are: first, whisky; second, tobacco; third, horses; fourth, guns; fifth, women.
Arapaho Indian proverb

It is absurd to argue from an analogy with wild animals and say that men and women ought to engage in the same occupations – for animals do not do housework.
Aristotle

There are only three things in the world that women do not understand – Liberty, Equality and Fraternity.
G K Chesterton

FREE WOMEN. Where?
Graffiti

It's only rarely that one can see in a little boy the promise of a man, but one can almost always see in a little girl the threat of a woman.　**Alexandre Dumas**

Women are sweetly-smiling people with pensive looks, innocent faces and cash-boxes for hearts.
Honoré de Balzac

Men who consistently leave the toilet seat up secretly want women to get up to go to the bathroom in the middle of the night and fall in.　**Rita Rudner**

It's amazing how many quick repairs a woman can fix with an ordinary kitchen knife, where a man can't lift a finger with his tool-chest.　**Tina Spencer Knott**

A woman is only a woman, but a good cigar is a smoke.　**Rudyard Kipling**

The only original thing about some men is original sin.
Helen Rowland

The woman whose behaviour indicates that she'll make a scene if she's told the truth asks to be deceived.
Elizabeth Jenkins

Beauty is all very well at first sight, but who ever looks at it when it has been in the house three days?
George Bernard Shaw

Nice men are never any good at getting taxis.
Katharine Whitehorn

I've never liked the expression 'Thinking Man's Crumpet'. Thinking Men shouldn't be *thinking* of crumpet.
Mary Mannion

A woman who strives to be like a man lacks ambition.
Helen Rowland

There is, of course, no reason for the existence of the male sex except that sometimes one needs help moving the piano.
Rebecca West

I still chase women – but only when they're running downhill.
Bob Hope

Ten years ago you could wink at a pretty girl, who would accept the implied compliment by sniffing, turning pink and saying, 'You chancer'. Do it today and you're a chauvinist pig.
Hugh Leonard

You don't take a sausage roll to a banquet.
Winston Churchill on why he didn't take his wife with him to an official function in Paris

One thing that feminism has taught me is that women are just as mean, basically, as we men are.
Norman Mailer

Mary had a little lamb. The gynaecologists are looking into it.
Graffiti

I'd have given ten conversations with Einstein for a first meeting with a pretty chorus girl.
Albert Camus

A woman must be a nice cuddly little thing: soft, sweet and stupid.   *Adolf Hitler*

Nature intended women to be our slaves. They belong to us just as a tree that bears fruit belongs to a gardener. What a mad idea to demand equality of the sexes. Women are nothing but machines for producing children.   *Napoleon*

Men don't understand anything about women and women understand nothing about men. And it's better that way.   *Vittorio Gassman*

I cannot bear men and women.   *George Bernard Shaw*

Dames are simple. I never met one who didn't understand a slap on the mouth.   *Humphrey Bogart*

No woman can love for longer than fifteen days, but I do not complain – they are delightful creatures.
                                              Rosanno Brazzi

Where young boys plan for *what* they will achieve and attain, young girls plan for *who* they will achieve and attain.   *Charlotte Gilman*

Women will be the weaker sex as long as they're strong enough to get away with it.   *Anon*

It's better to be unhappy alone than unhappy with someone else.   *Marilyn Monroe*

If the right man does not come along, there are many fates far worse. One is to have the *wrong* man come along.
Letitia Baldrige

The first time you buy a house you see how pretty the paint is. The second time you check up to see if the basement has termites. It's the same with men.
Lupe Velez

The only time a woman really succeeds in changing a man is when he's a baby.
Natalie Wood

The art of managing a man has to be learned from birth. It depends to some extent on one's distribution of curves.
Mary Hyde

Men don't really believe that women exist. Marilyn Monroe died of this.
Lucy Ellmann

A woman can walk through the Louvre Museum in Paris and see 5,000 breathtaking paintings on the wall. A man can walk through the Louvre Museum and see 5,000 nails in the wall. That's the difference between the sexes.
Erma Bombeck

Adam may have had his troubles, but he never had to listen to Eve talk about the other men she could have married.
Dom de Luise

There are three kinds of kissers: the fire extinguisher, the mummy and the vacuum cleaner. *Helen Gurley Brown*

A woman needs a man like a fish needs a bicycle.
Gloria Steinem

There are men I could spend eternity with. But not this life.
Kathleen Norris

It wasn't a woman who betrayed Jesus with a kiss.
Catherine Carswell

If a man does something silly, people say, 'Isn't he silly?' If a woman does something silly, people say, 'Aren't women silly?'
Doris Day

Women have a lot of faults, but men only two: everything they say and everything they do.
Leonora Strumpfenburg

More and more it appears that, biologically, men are destined for short brutal lives – and women for long, miserable ones.
Estelle Ramey

If men liked shopping, they'd call it research.
Cynthia Nelms

What's nice about my dating life is that I don't have to leave my house. All I have to do is read the paper. I'm marrying Richard Gere, dating Daniel Day-Lewis . . . Even Robert de Niro was in there for a day.
Julia Roberts

If you're a woman living, you've been done wrong by a man.
Oprah Winfrey

Men aren't attracted to me by my mind, they're attracted by what I *don't* mind. *Gypsy Rose Lee*

Macho doesn't prove mucho. *Zsa Zsa Gabor*

Most women need a room of their own – and often the only place to find it is outside their own homes. *Germaine Greer*

No matter what I go through, my girlfriend says she'll always be there for me. Unfortunately. *Art Hoskins*

Women should be obscene and not heard. *John Lennon*

I became a feminist as an alternative to becoming a masochist. *Sally Kempton*

Women spend a lot of time and energy minding men's egos. It's like living with a corn on your foot all the time. *Rhona Teehan*

It is delightful to be a woman, but every man thanks the Lord devoutly that he isn't one. *Olive Schreiner*

The man is a domestic animal which, if treated with firmness and kindness, can be trained to do most things. *Jilly Cooper*

When I met Mr Right I had no idea that his first name was Always. *Rita Rudner*

I was dating a guy for a while because he told me he had an incurable disease. I didn't realise it was stupidity.
Gracie Hart

The most important characteristic in a man for me? Breathing.
Joan Rivers

The reason men don't do laundry is because washing machines don't come with remote controls.
Erma Bombeck

By her seemingly effortless ability to be wrong about nearly everything, Andrea Dworkin is an essential guide to the culture and values of our time.
Declan Lynch

If you think women are the weaker sex, try pulling the blankets back to your side.
Stuart Turner

If there hadn't been women, we'd still be squatting in caves eating raw meat. We made civilisation to impress our girlfriends.
Orson Welles

A woman driver is one who drives like a man, and gets blamed for it.
Patricia Ledger

I once went out with a guy who asked me to mother him . . . so I spat on a hankie and wiped his face.
Jenny Jones

Like many women, I can't understand why every man who has ever changed a nappy has felt impelled, in recent years, to write a book about it.
Barbara Ehrenreich

Time and tide wait for no man, but time always stands still for a woman of thirty.   *Robert Frost*

It's because I never smoked, drank or touched a girl – until I was eleven years old.
                    George Moore on the reasons for his longevity

Man isn't the enemy. The real enemy is women's denigration of themselves.   *Betty Friedan*

MONEY

When a man says he wants to work, what he means is that he wants wages.   *Bishop Richard Whately*

A small loan makes a debtor, a large one an enemy.
                    Publilius Syrus

There is only one class in the community that thinks more about money than the rich, and that is the poor.
                    Oscar Wilde

The first test of a truly great man is his humility.
                    John Ruskin

When an actor has money he doesn't send letters, he sends telegrams.   *Anton Chekhov*

I worked my way up from nothing to a state of extreme poverty.   *Groucho Marx*

Income is an amount of money that, no matter how large it is, you spend more than.

Ed Asner

The best time for me is when I don't have any problems I can't buy my way out of.

Andy Warhol

I want a man who only has to be kind and understanding. Is that too much to ask of a multi-millionaire?

Zsa Zsa Gabor

Three things have helped me successfully through the ordeals of life – an understanding husband, a good analyst . . . and millions and millions of dollars.

Mary Tyler Moore

No entrepreneur I know is motivated by money. It's the idea; seeing how far you can go.

Anita Roddick

There are three ways to lose money: on horses, women and engineers. Horses are the easiest, women the most fun and engineers the fastest.

Rolf Skar

Man does not live by GNP alone.

Paul Samuelson

The meek shall inherit the earth, but not the mineral rights.

J Paul Getty

If you would know what the Lord thinks of money, you have only to look at those to whom he gives it.

Maurice Baring

The misfortune of the wise is better than the
prosperity of the fool.   *Epicurus*

Wealth is not only what we have, but what we *are*.
                                            Anon

Anyone who lives within his means suffers from a lack
of imagination.   *Lionel Stander*

Everything I owe, I owe because of my wife.
                                  Donald Trump

A rich man is nothing but a poor man with money.
                                      W C Fields

It is only the poor who are forbidden to beg.
                                  Anatole France

Greed is good.   *Stanley Weiser*

One must be poor to know the luxury of giving.
                                    George Eliot

Love lasteth as long as the money endureth.
                                  William Caxton

Poverty is the parent of revolution and crime.   *Aristotle*

Money is like an arm or leg. Use it or lose it.
                                      Henry Ford

Spendthrifts make their heirs prematurely grey.
                                      Hal Roach

Retirement is twice the husband on half the money.
Sean McCarthy

Saving is a very fine thing. Especially when your parents have done it for you. **Winston Churchill**

Money won't create success, the freedom to make it will. **Nelson Mandela**

I've never been poor, only broke. Being poor is a frame of mind: being broke is a temporary situation.
Mike Todd

To be clever enough to get all that money, one must be stupid enough to want it. **G K Chesterton**

I'd like to be so rich I could throw soap away after the letters had worn off. **Andy Rooney**

No one would remember the Good Samaritan if he *only* had good intentions . . . he had money as well.
Margaret Thatcher

All decent people live beyond their means nowadays, and those who aren't respectable live beyond other people's. A few gifted individuals manage to do both.
Saki

Anyone who has ever struggled with poverty knows how devilishly expensive it is to be poor. **James Baldwin**

My mother's idea of economy was to take a bus ride to the Ritz. **Lady Trumpington**

I would not say millionaires were mean. They simply have a healthy respect for money. I've noticed that people who don't respect money don't have any.

J Paul Getty

I went in search of a one-armed economist so that the guy could never make a statement and then say, 'but on the other hand . . .'

President Harry Truman

Love your husband. Trust your husband. But get everything in your own name.

Joan Rivers

A man can be forgiven a lot if he can quote Shakespeare in an economic crisis.

Philip, Duke of Edinburgh

A deficit is what you have when you haven't as much as when you had nothing.

Ambrose Bierce

The criterion of a gentleman is that however poor he may be he still refuses to do useful work.

George Mikes

Live within your income – even if you have to borrow to do so.

Josh Billings

Gambling is the surest way of getting nothing for something.

Wilson Mizner

The ideal job is one for which you are paid large sums for doing nothing at all.

Alan Coren

I cried all the way to the bank.
Liberace on how he dealt with critics of his music

Anything that won't sell I don't want to invent.
Thomas Edison

If God hadn't intended us to gamble, he would never have given us money. *Zsa Zsa Gabor*

If all the rich people in the world divided up their money among themselves, there wouldn't be enough to go round. *Christina Stead*

I don't invest in anything I don't understand. It makes more sense to buy TV stations than oil wells.
Oprah Winfrey

Those who have money think that the most important thing in the world is love. The poor know it is money.
Gerald Brenan

Kissing your hand may make you feel very good, but a diamond and sapphire bracelet lasts for ever. *Anita Loos*

When I was young I used to think that wealth and power could bring me happiness – I was right.
Gahan Wilson

Someone once said to me that The Beatles were anti-materialistic. That's a huge myth. John and I literally used to sit down and say, 'Now, let's write a swimming pool'. *Paul McCartney*

If you can actually count your money you're not really a rich man.   *J Paul Getty*

I've done the most unutterable rubbish just for money. The lure of the zeros was simply too great.
                                          Richard Burton

Money is like sex. You think of nothing else if you don't have it, and other things if you do.   *James Baldwin*

There are three kinds of economists: those who can count and those who can't.   *Eddie George*

He's a fool that makes his doctor his heir.
                                          Benjamin Franklin

A poor relation is the most irrelevant thing in nature.
                                          Charles Lamb

An acquaintance is someone we know well enough to borrow money from but not to lend to.   *Hal Roach*

You never realise how short a month is until you have to pay alimony.   *John Barrymore*

Put not your trust in money, but put your money in trust.   *Oliver Wendell Holmes*

When somebody says 'It ain't the money but the principle of the thing', it's the money.   *Elbert Hubbard*

Extravagant restaurants should have at least one table
where you can starve at reasonable prices.

Herbert Prochnow

You should go on living just to annoy those who are
paying your annuities.

Voltaire

Money can't buy happiness. That's why we have credit
cards.

Red Skelton

The hardest thing in the world to understand is
income tax.

Albert Einstein

Don't lend money to a man who runs his office from a
phone booth.

Rita Rudner

Any man who has $10,000 when he dies is a failure.

Errol Flynn

A bank is a place where they lend you an umbrella in
fine weather and then ask for it back again when it
begins to rain.

Robert Frost

Pennies don't come from heaven. They have to be
earned here on earth.

Margaret Thatcher

The wretchedness of being rich is that you have to live
with rich people.

Logan Pearsall Smith

Don't go into a bank if the man in front of you is
wearing a balaclava.

Kevin McAleer

A successful man is one who earns more than his wife can spend. A successful woman is one who marries a successful man.
Lana Turner

Buying what you don't need leads to needing what you can't buy.
Hilaire Belloc

Banks used to frown on you if you tried to spend more than you had. Now they frown on you if you *don't*.
Lambert Jeffries

The answer to 99 out of 100 questions in life is money.
Cameron Crowe

Women prefer men who have something tender about them – particularly the legal kind.
Kay Ingram

An accountant is a man you hired to explain that you didn't earn the money you did.
Ellen Westwood

There are two rules about life. One is that the sun will rise in the east. Rule Two states that as long as there are rich men trying not to feel old there will be young girls trying not to feel poor.
Julie Birchill

Christmas is a time when we spend money we don't have on things we don't need to impress people we don't like.
Jill Johnston

I spent so much on my girlfriend I decided to marry her for my money.
Richard Pryor

Just because it's put on the account doesn't mean it costs less.
Anthony Powell

In all recorded history, there hasn't been one economist who's had to worry about where the next meal was coming from.
Peter Drucker

A man who has a million dollars is as well off as if he were rich.
J Paul Getty

Misers believe in letting the rest of the world go buy.
Louis Safian

The earth is about 5,000 million years old. Who can afford to live in the past?
Harold Pinter

I never turned over a fig leaf that didn't have a price tag on the other side.
Saul Bellow

Money is better than poverty, if only for financial reasons.
Woody Allen

Few rich men own their own property. The property owns them.
Robert Ingersoll

Running into debt isn't half as bad as running into creditors.
Brendan Grace

A bargain is something that's no use, but it's so cheap you can't afford not to buy it.
Herbert Prochnow

A consultant is someone who knows less about your business than you, but who gets more out of it by telling you what he knows than you do if you make it work the right way instead of doing what he tells you.

Denis Greig

When opportunity knocks, make sure they're not looking for VAT.

Graffiti

We'd all like a reputation for generosity, and we'd all like to buy it cheap.

Mignon McLaughlin

If you think supporting your wife is expensive, try *not* supporting her.

Sid Caesar

People who think money can do anything may very well be suspected of doing anything for money.

Mary Pettibone Poole

If all economists were laid end to end, they would not reach a conclusion.

George Bernard Shaw

At fat farms and beauty spas, one pays astronomical sums to be over-exercised and under-fed.

Peg Bracken

There must be more to life than having everything.

Maurice Sendak

Poverty keeps together more homes than it breaks up.

Saki

Education is a wonderful thing. If you couldn't sign your name you'd have to pay cash.

Rita Mae Brown

Mother always said that honesty was the best policy and money wasn't everything. She was wrong about other things too.
Gerald Barzan

Divorce lawyers only referee the fight, but they still end up with the purse.
Johnny Carson

The middle classes wear last year's suit and drive this year's car on next year's income.
Herbert Prochnow

The main difference between men and boys is that men's toys cost more money.
Kevin Goldstein-Jackson

If you've ever really been poor, you remain so at heart all your life.
Arnold Bennett

The trouble with being poor is that it takes up all of your time.
Ogden Nash

If someone is dumb enough to offer me a million dollars a picture, I'm not dumb enough to refuse it.
Elizabeth Taylor

If you would know the value of money, go and try to borrow some.
Benjamin Franklin

If you pay peanuts, you get monkeys.
James Goldsmith

Buy old masters. They fetch a much better price than old mistresses.
Lord Beaverbrook

All heiresses are beautiful.
John Dryden

My conscience is fine. It's my pay that needs rising.
Phyllis Diller

If I was as rich as people say, I wouldn't have gone to Vietnam: I'd have *sent* for it.
Bob Hope

Making money is art and working is art and good business is the best art of all.
Andy Warhol

If the package doesn't say '*new*', these days, it better say '*ten cents off*'.
Spencer Klaw

I couldn't imagine anything duller than a man with a regular income. I find financial insecurity a great aphrodisiac.
Marian Keyes

Contempt for wealth is a trick used by the rich to keep the poor without it.
Mario Puzo

A fool and his money are soon parted. What I want to know is how they got together in the first place.
Cyril Fletcher

I've been rich and I've been poor. Believe me – rich is better.
Sophie Tucker

Get money first; virtue comes afterwards.
Horace

Money is a good thing to have. It frees you from doing things you dislike. Since I dislike doing practically *everything*, that's why I like it so much.
Groucho Marx

After a certain point in time, money is meaningless. It ceases to be the goal. The game is what counts.

Aristotle Onassis

Always try to rub up against money. If you do it long enough, some of it may rub off on you.   *Damon Runyon*

A son can bear with equanimity the loss of a father, but the loss of his inheritance may drive him to despair.

Machiavelli

The quickest way to find long-lost friends is to win a fortune in the lottery.   *Kevin Goldstein-Jackson*

Not having to worry about money is like not having to worry about dying.   *Mario Puzo*

OPTIMISTS & PESSIMISTS

A pessimist looks both ways when crossing a one-way street.

An optimist leaves the car engine running while his wife buys a hat.

A pessimist discounts his blessings.

An optimist thinks that when his shoes wear out he'll be back on his feet.

A pessimist says business conditions are as bad as they could be – and will probably get worse.

An optimist sees 'o' as the first letter in 'opportunity'.

A pessimist sees it as the last letter in 'zero'.

An optimist laughs to forget.

A pessimist forgets to laugh.

An optimist is someone who hasn't got around to reading the daily paper.

A pessimist believes it's euphemistic.

An optimist is someone who gets treed by a lion and enjoys the scenery.

A pessimist is someone who's been forced to live with an optimist.

An optimist believes in the best of all possible worlds.

A pessimist *fears* we do.

An optimist believes Sylvester Stallone won't make any more movies.

A pessimist doesn't get out of the bath to answer the phone.

An optimist starts a crossword with a fountain pen.

A pessimist keeps an optimist from becoming smug.

An optimist saves the seed catalogues to compare with the flowers he actually grows.

A pessimist who smells flowers looks for the coffin.

An optimist reaches for the car keys when the after-dinner speaker says, 'And finally . . .'

A pessimist is an optimist in full possession of the facts.

An optimist thinks the empty space beside the kerb won't have a 'No Parking' sign on it.

If it wasn't for the pessimist, the optimist wouldn't realise how happy he was.

PARENTS & CHILDREN

An ugly baby is a very nasty object – and the prettiest is frightful.
Queen Victoria

How do I cope with my children? I have a big house . . . and I hide a lot.
Mary Ure

Remember that as a teenager you're at the last stage in your life when you'll be happy to hear the phone is for you.
Fran Lebowitz

Children, not having yet learnt how to be hypocritical, are quite frank about pointing out their own merits.
Virginia Graham

Have you ever had that sneaking feeling that shopkeepers don't like children?
Serena Allott

All those writers who wrote about their childhood. Gentle God, if I wrote about mine, you wouldn't sit in the same room with me.
Dorothy Parker

A psychiatrist said, 'Be careful in the way you discipline your children or you could permanently damage their Id'. Damage it? I didn't even know where it was. For all I knew, it either made you sterile or caused dandruff. Once I suspected where it was, I made the kid wear four diapers just to be safe.
Erma Bombeck

I love all my children – but some of them I don't like.
Lillian Carter

If you've never been hated by your children, you've never been a parent.
Bette Davis

There's nothing worse than a man with a cold. He thinks he's dying. I always wonder how they'd survive childbirth.
Miriam O'Callaghan

Perfection is terrible: it cannot have children.

Sylvia Plath

Adults are always asking little kids what they want to be when they grow up – they're obviously looking for ideas.

Paula Poundstone

You see much more of your children once they leave home.

Lucille Ball

I asked my old man if I could go ice-skating on the lake. He said, 'Wait till it gets warmer'.

Rodney Dangerfield

I want to have children and I know my time is running out. I want to have them while my parents are still young enough to take care of them.

Rita Rudner

Children today only know two words: 'No' and 'Wallet'.

Jasper Carrott

Our son kept our marriage together. Neither of us wanted custody of him.

Roy 'Chubby' Brown

It takes a woman 20 years to make a man out of her son – and another woman 20 minutes to make a fool out of him.

Helen Rowland

I would have made a terrible mother. For one thing, I hate to repeat myself.

Joan Manley

The only time a woman wishes she were a year older is when she's expecting a baby.   *Mary Marsh*

The real menace in dealing with a five-year-old is that in no time at all you begin to sound like a five-year-old.
Jean Kerr

Good parents, when they realise they're guilt-tripping their kids, will stop themselves in mid-whine.
Cynthia Heimel

I knew I was an unwanted child when I saw that my new bath toys were a toaster and a radio.   *Joan Rivers*

I'm a virgin and I brought up all my children to be the same.   *Shirley Bassey*

Don't bother discussing sex with small children. They rarely have anything to add.   *Fran Lebowitz*

The young are generally full of revolt, and are often pretty revolting about it.   *Mignon McLaughlin*

Don't have any children. It makes divorce so much more complicated.   *Albert Einstein*

Other species have the good sense to banish their young at an early age.   *John Rae*

The fundamental defect of fathers in our competitive society is that they want their children to be a credit to them.   *Bertrand Russell*

Anyone who hates children and animals can't be all bad.
W C Fields

A teenager is an old person with sixty years deducted.
Pat Ingoldsby

The main trouble with children is that they're not returnable.
Quentin Crisp

All women become like their mothers. That is their tragedy. No man does. That's his.
Oscar Wilde

It's no wonder people are so horrible when we consider the fact that they started life as children.
Kingsley Amis

It's not the stork in the morning that brings the babies – it's the lark at night.
Herbert Prochnow

My children never forgave me. Oedipus killed his father and married his mother, but I sold their Nintendo.
Sue Arnold

Having a baby is like trying to push a grand piano through a transom.
Alice Roosevelt Longworth

It's funny that the two things most men are proudest of are the things that any man can do – be drunk and be the father of their son.
Gertrude Stein

I come from a typical American family. Me, my mother, her third husband, his daughter from a second marriage, her stepsister, her illegitimate son.
Carol Henry

If you're doing your job properly, your children must walk away from you.   *Josephine Hart*

A normal adolescent isn't a normal adolescent if he acts normal.   *Judith Viorst*

One thing they never tell you about child-rearing is that for the rest of your life, at the drop of a hat, you're expected to know your child's name and how old he or she is.   *Erma Bombeck*

A liberal mother is someone who worries when her daughter comes home *early* from a date.   *Fran Lebowitz*

There are only two things a child will share willingly – communicable diseases and his mother's age.   *Benjamin Spock*

The easiest way for your children to learn about money is for you not to have any.   *Katharine Whitehorn*

Don't become a father 18 years before a war.   *E B White*

There are no illegitimate children, only illegitimate parents.   *Maeve Kennedy*

There's a time when you have to explain to your children why they're born – and it's a marvellous thing if you know by then.   *Hazel Scott*

Youth would be an ideal state if it came a little later in life.   *Lord Asquith*

We are the people our mothers warned us against.

John Lennon

I believe in large families. Every woman should have at least three husbands.

Zsa Zsa Gabor

Never have ideas about children, and never have ideas *for* them.

George Orwell

The main purpose of children's parties is to remind you that there are kids in the world even more awful than your own.

Katharine Whitehorn

If God had meant men to have children, he would have given them pvc aprons.

Victoria Wood

I wasn't loved as a child. One day my mother said to me, 'Why can't you be more like Sheila?' Sheila died at birth.

Joan Rivers

Most of us become parents long before we have stopped being children.

Mignon McLaughlin

Why do grandparents and grandchildren get along so well? Because they have the same enemy – the mother.

Claudette Colbert

As a breastfeeding mother, you're basically just meals on heels.

Kathy Lette

Sometimes being a mother really stinks. I'm in charge because I'm the oldest and the biggest, but there's no book of instructions.

Cher

Every family should have at least three children. Then if one of them turns out to be a genius, the other two can support him.
George Carlin

The truth is that it is not the sins of the fathers that descend unto the third generation, but the sorrows of the mothers.
Marilyn French

The way I figure it is this: if the kids are still alive by the time my husband comes home, I've done my job.
Roseanne

The next time I'm not just having an epidural for the birth – I'm having one for the conception as well.
Sally James

To be the father of a nation is a great honour but to be the father of a family is even a greater joy.
Nelson Mandela

One of the things I've discovered about children is that they don't really give a damn about the fact that you walked five miles to school.
Patty Duke

With the birth of each child you lose two novels.
Candida McWilliam

The great secret of dealing successfully with an adolescent is not to have one.
James Simpson

Children should be seen and not smelt.
Joyce Jillson

Home is where the DVD is.
Graffiti

We spend the first twelve months of our children's lives teaching them to walk and talk, and the next twelve telling them to sit down and shut up.   *Phyllis Diller*

A food isn't necessarily healthy because your child hates it.   *Katharine Whitehorn*

Do not allow your children to mix drinks. It's unseemly – and they use too much vermouth.
Fran Lebowitz

Everybody knows how to raise children except the people who have them.   *P J O'Rourke*

To be a successful father there's one absolute rule: when you have a kid, don't look at it for the first two years.   *Ernest Hemingway*

You know you're trailer trash when you allow your 12 year old daughter to smoke at the dinner table in front of all her kids.   *Greta Garbage*

I only saw him twice and we have two children.
Sheilah Graham

I knew I was funny the minute I was born. All the nurses started laughing.   *Mel Brooks*

The best thing that could happen to motherhood already has: fewer women are going into it.
Victoria Billings

The quickest way for a parent to get a child's attention is to sit down and look comfortable.   *Lena Olinghouse*

Children's talent to endure stems from their ignorance of alternatives.   *Maya Angelou*

A man in a delivery room is about as helpful as a nun at a bar mitzvah.   *Rita Rudner*

The best way to keep children in the house is to create a harmonious atmosphere – and let the air out of their car tyres.   *Dorothy Parker*

The worst misfortune that can happen to an ordinary man is to have an extraordinary father.   *Austin O'Malley*

Parents are people who practise the rhythm method of birth control.   *Peter O'Toole*

My husband and I have discovered a foolproof method of birth control: an hour with the kids before bedtime.   *Roseanne*

Setting a good example for your child takes all the fun out of middle age.   *William Faulkner*

If men had to have babies, they'd only have one each.   *Princess Diana*

If one is not going to take the necessary precautions to avoid having parents, one must undertake to bring them up.   *Quentin Crisp*

Because of their size, parents are very difficult to discipline.

P J O'Rourke

The only way to stop children from nagging to be taken to Disneyland is either to go or strangle them.

Jeff Coren

It puzzles me how a child can see a dairy bar 3 miles away, but he cannot see a 4 by 6 rug that has scrunched up under his feet and has been dragged through two rooms.

Erma Bombeck

My mother loved children. She would have given anything for me to be one.

Groucho Marx

There are three ways to get something done – do it yourself, hire someone, or forbid your kids to do it.

Monta Crane

You can tell a child is growing up when he stops asking where he came from and refuses to say where he's going.

Joan O'Donoghue

Never raise your hand to your children – it leaves your mid-section unprotected.

Robert Orpen

If you can't afford suppositories for your kids, a good cure for constipation is to sit them on the lavvy and tell them ghost stories.

Roy 'Chubby' Brown

More twins are being born these days because babies are afraid to come into the world alone.

Herbert Prochnow

Do not, on a rainy day, ask your child what he feels like doing, because I can assure you that it is not something you'll feel like watching. *Fran Lebowitz*

A mother never realises that her children are no longer children. *Holbrook Jackson*

You can't expect a boy to be vicious until he's been to a really good school. *Saki*

Every time a child says 'I don't believe in fairies', a little fairy somewhere falls down dead. *J M Barrie*

A child becomes an adult when he realises he has a right not only to be right but also to be wrong. *Thomas Szasz*

Children have never been very good at listening to their elders, but they have never failed to imitate them. *James Baldwin*

Every child should have an occasional pat on the back, as long as it is applied hard enough. *Fulton Sheen*

Cleaning your house while the kids are growing is like shovelling the walk before it stops snowing. *Phyllis Diller*

It's all any reasonable child can expect if the dad is present at the conception. *Joe Orton*

The first half of our lives is ruined by our parents and the second by our children. *Clarence Darrow*

Every generation revolts against its father and makes friends with its grandfathers. *Lewis Mumford*

The mother of the year should be a sterilised woman with two adopted children. *Paul Ehrlich*

Few misfortunes can befall a boy which bring worse consequences than to have a really affectionate mother. *W Somerset Maugham*

The best way to give advice to your kids is to find out what they want and tell them to do it. *Harry Truman*

The best time to put children to bed is whenever they go. *Fran Lebowitz*

I wanted to change the world but I couldn't find a babysitter. *Feminist graffiti*

The thing that impresses me most about America is the way parents obey their children. *Edward VIII*

The value of marriage is not that adults produce children, but that children produce adults. *Peter de Vries*

A mother isn't a person to lean on, but one who makes leaning unnecessary. *Dorothy Fisher*

The only things that teenagers wear out quicker than shoes are parents.

James Simpson

PEOPLE & PLACES

Never again shall it be that this beautiful land will again experience the oppression of one by another and suffer the indignity of being the skunk of the world.

Nelson Mandela in his inauguration speech in 1994

Rome reminds me of a man who lives by exhibiting to travellers his grandmother's corpse.

James Joyce

Beer is the Danish national drink, and the Danish national weakness is another beer.

Clementine Paddleford

God, what on earth was I drinking last night? My head feels like there's a Frenchman living in it.

Ben Elton

From every Englishman emanates a kind of gas, the deadly choke-damp of boredom.

Heinrich Heine

In America only the successful writer is important. In France all writers are important, in England no writer is important, and in Australia you have to explain what a writer is.

Geoffrey Cotterel

When a boy is bored with Glasgow he is ready to live.

Ian Pattison

I find it hard to say, because when I was there, it seemed to be shut.
Barry Humphries after being asked if he liked New Zealand

Americans like fat books and thin women.
Russell Baker

Of all people in the world, the English have the least sense of the beauty of literature. *Oscar Wilde*

Dublin used to be one of the prettiest cities in Europe and now it's a shambolical mess. *Bob Geldof*

American women expect to find in their husbands a perfection that English women only hope to find in their butlers. *W Somerset Maugham*

An Englishman thinks he is moral when he is only uncomfortable. *George Bernard Shaw*

Very little is known of the Canadian country since it is rarely visited by anyone but the Queen and illiterate sport fishermen. *P J O'Rourke*

Being a woman is like being Irish. Everyone says you're important and nice but you still take second place all the time. *Iris Murdoch*

The English are polite by telling lies, Americans by telling the truth. *Malcolm Bradbury*

The great nations have always acted like gangsters and the small ones like prostitutes.   *Stanley Kubrick*

The only justification for railway timetables is to let passengers know how late their trains are going to be.
Kevin Goldstein-Jackson

An Englishman's real ambition is to get a railway compartment to himself.   *Ian Hay*

Everything in France is a pretext for a good dinner.
Jean Anouilh

An Irishman is only at peace when he's fighting.
Brendan Behan

There are no second acts in American lives.
F Scott Fitzgerald

Never remark in England that the air in Ireland is excellent for they will surely tax it.   *Jonathan Swift*

A gifted person ought to learn English in thirty hours, French in thirty days and German in thirty years.
Mark Twain

I wanted to play the bright young Irish, so I came to London.   *Sean Hughes*

Done the elephants, done the poverty. Nothing left to do.   *Phil Tufnell after a few days in India*

An Irish alibi is proof that you were in two places at one time.
Anthony Butler

Englishmen think over a compliment for a week so that by the time they pay it, it is addled like a bad egg.
W J Locke

In America you can buy a lifetime's supply of aspirin for one dollar – and use it all up in two weeks.
John Barrymore

The English never draw a line without blurring it.
Winston Churchill

The crime situation is so bad in some American cities, you could walk five blocks and never leave the scene of the crime.
E C McKenzie

I was at the library today. The librarian asked me for proof that I was a citizen of New York, so I stabbed him.
Emo Philips

I never met anyone in Ireland who understood the Irish question except one Englishman who had only been there a week.
Keith Fraser

The Irish don't know what they want, and are prepared to fight to the death to get it.
Sidney Littlewood

My generation of Canadians grew up believing that, if we were very good or very smart, or both, we would some day graduate from Canada.
Robert Fulford

Ireland will put a shillelagh into orbit, Israel will put a matzo ball into orbit, and Lichtenstein will put a postage stamp into orbit before the Canadians ever put up a mouse.
Brendan Behan

Even stupid people in Britain are smarter than Americans.
Madonna

The English find ill-health not only interesting but respectable, and often experience death in an effort to avoid a fuss.
Pamela Franklin

New York is the only city where people make radio requests like, 'This is for Tina. I'm sorry I stabbed you.'
Carol Liefer

In Tulsa, the restaurants have signs that say, 'Sorry, we're open'.
Roseanne

If you never want to see a man again, say 'I love you. I want to marry you. I want your children.' They leave skid marks.
Rita Rudner

It takes a great deal to produce *ennui* in an Englishman, and if you do, he only takes it as convincing proof that you are well-bred.
Margaret Halsey

The Jews invented guilt and the Irish turned it into an art form.
Walter Matthau

Nobody is healthy in London. Nobody can be.

Jane Austen

You know how the French see the English – drunk in charge of a limited vocabulary and a lager can.

Alan Bleasdale

The Welsh are nothing more than Italians in the rain.

Elaine Morgan

The English woman is so refined.
She has no bosom and no behind.

Stevie Smith

In Russia a man is called reactionary if he objects to having his property stolen and his wife and children murdered.

Winston Churchill

A large poster headed 'Man Wanted For Murder' was placed outside a Glasgow police station . . . and 200 men applied for the job.

Stanley Baxter

Americans are too clean to revolt. They spend all their time changing their shirts and washing themselves. You can't feel fierce and revolutionary in the bathroom.

Eric Linklater

I didn't want to move to the Midwest. I could never live in a place where the outstanding geographical feature is the horizon.

George Carlin

There's no place like Ireland. It's a place where the Stone Age is literally still there, but they have cable TV and cell phones.

Frank Gannon

A German joke is no laughing matter.   *Mark Twain*

I like Milwaukee. I go there every year for a sensory deprivation experiment.   *Emo Philips*

Only Americans have mastered the art of being prosperous and broke at the same time.   *E C McKenzie*

When it's 3 o'clock in New York, it's still 1938 in London.   *Bette Midler*

American men as a group are only interested in two things: money and breast.   *Hedy Lamarr*

The English think of an opinion as something which a decent person, if he has the misfortune to have one, does all he can to hide.   *Margaret Halsey*

There are worse places than Hastings. Beirut and Sarajevo spring to mind.   *Jo Brand*

Melbourne is the kind of town that makes you ask the question, 'Is there life before death?'   *Bette Midler*

As far as America is concerned, respect for the artist is at about the same level as for the waste matter of a dog last Monday in Hyde Park.   *Rod Steiger*

An Irishman can be worried by the thought that there's nothing to worry about.   *Austin O'Malley*

It was wonderful to find America but it would have been more wonderful to miss it. *Mark Twain*

In America, sex is an obsession. In other parts of the world it is a fact. *Marlene Dietrich*

Nobody goes to the theatre in England unless they have bronchitis. *James Agate*

America has plenty of good five cent cigars. But they charge fifteen cents for them. *Will Rogers*

No matter how politely or distinctly you ask a Parisian a question, he will persist in answering you in French. *Fran Lebowitz*

American water is so dirty, many of our fish are beaching themselves and asking for asylum. *Bob Hope*

England will never be civilised until she has added Utopia to her dominions. *Oscar Wilde*

The Englishman has all the qualities of a poker, except its occasional warmth. *Daniel O'Connell*

Realising that they will never be a world power, the Cypriots have decided to be a world nuisance instead. *George Mikes*

I am willing to love all mankind, except an American. *Samuel Johnson*

A nation is a society united by a delusion about its ancestry and a common hatred of its neighbours.

William Inge

Cusins is a very nice fellow, certainly: nobody would ever guess that he was born in Australia.

George Bernard Shaw

The trouble with America is that there are far too many wide open spaces – surrounded by teeth.

Charles Luckman

America is the only nation in history which has gone directly from barbarism to decadence without the customary intervening period of civilisation.

Georges Clemenceau

In Ireland there's a precedence for everything except common sense.

Ben Kiely

The English have a miraculous power of turning wine into water.

Oscar Wilde

Time has confirmed Shakespeare as the wisest of Englishmen, an admittedly handicapped contest.

Frank Gannon

Waiting for the German verb is surely the ultimate thrill.

Flann O'Brien

Frustrate a Frenchman and he will drink himself to death. Frustrate an Irishman and he will die of hypertension. A Dane will shoot himself while an American will get drunk, shoot *you*, and then establish a million dollar aid programme for your relatives.

Stuart Rudin

It's an American characteristic not to stop running even after you've arrived.

Clive James

In England people actually try to be brilliant at breakfast. That is so dreadful of them! Only dull people are brilliant at breakfast.

Oscar Wilde

If it was raining soup, the Irish would be out with forks.

Brendan Behan

Germany is a great nation only because its people have so much Polish blood in their veins.

Friedrich Nietzsche

The US is like the guy at the party who gives cocaine to everybody and still nobody likes him.

Jim Samuels

New York is made out of modelling clay.

Truman Capote

A country as devoted to the condom as Holy Communion.

Pól ó Conghaile on Italy

If you stay here much longer, you're going to go back with slitty eyes.

Prince Philip to a student at a reception during a visit to Peking in 1986

I am terribly blunt, having been raised in the English tradition which permits a gentleman to be almost infinitely rude, provided he keeps his voice down.
Raymond Chandler

Gina Lollobrigida is the most publicised aspect of Italian life since Nero stopped throwing Christians to the lions.
Tom Wiseman

You don't die in the United States. You just under-achieve.
Jerzy Kozinski

When passing for Irish, you're advised to go easy on the deodorant and the shampoo. Dandruff is de rigueur.
Sean Kelly

English plays are like English puddings: nobody has any taste for them but themselves.
Voltaire

What really got me about America was the plentitude of all-night walk-in taxidermy stores. How convenient.
Billy Connolly

A riddle wrapped in a mystery inside an enigma.
Winston Churchill on Russia

It is absurd to say there are neither ruins nor curiosities in America when they have their mothers and their accents.
Oscar Wilde

The only interesting thing than can happen in a Swiss bedroom is suffocation by a feather mattress.
Dalton Trumbo

The ignorance of French society gives one a rough sense of the infinite. *Joseph Renan*

Americans are crazy people. They treat cigarette smokers like villainous carriers of the Black Death, and yet every home is a virtual arsenal, bulging with handguns. Babes from birth suck on the teated muzzles of .38 revolvers and are trained to perforate anyone who might call to the wrong address after nightfall. *Hugh Leonard*

Continental people have a sex life. The English have hot water bottles. *George Mikes*

I can't have any respect for a country whose evolution stopped with the mousse. *Tommy Tiernan on Canada*

The term Great Britain is an oxymoron. *Ardal O'Hanlon*

Belfast is a hard and cruel town inhabited by people who, due to bad planning on the part of whatever passes for a Creator, happen to live next door to each other. *Gerry Anderson*

The French invented the only known cure for dandruff. It's called the guillotine. *P G Wodehouse*

Guilt isn't an emotion in the Celtic countries; it's simply a way of life – a kind of gleefully painful social anaesthetic. *A L Kennedy*

Other people have a nationality. The Irish and the Jews
have a *psychosis*. **Brendan Behan**

The national sport of Australia is breaking furniture,
and the average daily consumption of beer in Sydney is
ten and three quarter imperial gallons for children
under the age of nine. **P J O'Rourke**

An Englishman does everything on principle: he fights
you on patriotic principles; he robs you on business
principles; he enslaves you on imperial principles.
George Bernard Shaw

Are you Indian or Pakistani? I can never tell the
difference between you chaps. **Prince Philip**

A friend of mine, during his occasional dark night of
the soul, is much given to declaring that if Ireland is
ever given an enema, Roscrea is where they will stick
the tube. Personally, I think there are far worse places
than Roscrea, a town which I spent an enchanting 24
hours one lunchtime. **Hugh Leonard**

America is where the wildest humans on the planet
came to do anything they damn well pleased.
P J O'Rourke

A man who is tired of London is tired of life? No, I
was tired of hunting for parking spaces. **Paul Theroux**

The English always have their wars in someone else's
country. **Brendan Behan**

PHILOSOPHICAL SPECULATIONS

To be free is not merely to cast off one's chains, but to live in a way that respects and enhances the freedom of others.
Nelson Mandela

Mankind must put an end to war, or war will put an end to mankind.
John F Kennedy

People are able because they *think* they're able.
Virgil

A big man has no time really to do anything but just sit and be big.
Scott Fitzgerald

He who never climbed high never fell low.
Thomas Fuller

If I'm such a legend, why am I so lonely?
Judy Garland

No really great man ever thought himself so.
William Hazlitt

Reality is merely an illusion, albeit a very persistent one.
Albert Einstein

What if everything is an illusion and nothing exists? Then I definitely paid too much for my carpet.
Woody Allen

There's no record in human history of a happy philosopher.
H L Mencken

If your head says one thing and your whole life says another, your head always loses. *Maxwell Anderson*

When one has been threatened with a great injustice, one accepts a smaller one as a favour. *Jane Welsh*

The human race has improved everything except the human race. *Adlai Stevenson*

We are never so happy nor so unhappy as we imagine. *La Rochefoucauld*

Progress was all right, but it went on too long. *James Thurber*

There's only one true philosophical problem – suicide. *Albert Camus*

An eye for an eye makes the whole world blind. *Gandhi*

Imagination is more important than knowledge. *Albert Einstein*

Being a philosopher, I have a problem for every solution. *Robert Zend*

We have to lose our mind to come to our senses. *Frederick Perls*

The most distressing thing that can happen to a prophet is to be proved wrong. The second most distressing thing is to be proved right. *Aldous Huxley*

People who think they're happy should rummage
through their dreams.   *Edward Dahlberg*

The most wasted day is that in which we have not
laughed.   *Sebastian Chamfort*

We can forgive those who bore us. We cannot forgive
those whom we bore.   *La Rochfoucald*

POLITICS

In my country we go to prison first and then become
President.   *Nelson Mandela*

Every man should have a wife because there are some
things you can't blame on the government.   *Hal Roach*

In a democracy you can say what you like as long as
you do what you're told.   *Anthony Butler*

The cheapest way to have your family tree traced is to
go into politics.   *Bob Hope*

Democracy is too good to share with just anybody.
                                         H L Mencken

It is not known that men enter local politics solely as a
result of being unhappily married.   *C Northcote Parkinson*

A politician is a person who has nothing to say but
says it anyway.   *Sean Hughes*

The wrong sort of people are always in power because they would not be in power if they were not the wrong sort of people. *Jon Wynne-Tyson*

All terrorists, at the invitation of the Government, end up with drinks at the Dorchester. *Hugh Gaitskell*

When a politician says yes he means maybe. When he says maybe he means no, and when he says no he's no politician. When a lady says no she means maybe. When she says maybe she means yes, but when she says yes she's no lady. *Edwina Currie*

A throne is only a bench covered with velvet. *Napoleon*

A communist is a socialist in a violent hurry. *G W Gough*

Politics offers yesterday's solutions to today's problems. *Marshall McLuhan*

A government that's big enough to give you what you want is big enough to take it all away. *Barry Goldwater*

A conservative is someone who demands a square deal for the rich. *David Frost*

She took the country off the landowners and gave it to the estate agents. *Denis Healey on Margaret Thatcher*

I have played football since I was a toddler. Left wing, as you would expect. *Robert Maxwell*

Bureaucracy defends the status quo long after the quo
has lost its status.
Laurence J Peter

The last person who went into the House of
Commons with good intentions was Guy Fawkes.
Alfred Wintle

Politics is for people who are too ugly to get into
showbusiness.
Bill Clinton

Ronald Reagan thought arms control was a kind of
deodorant.
Patricia Schroeder

If Kitchener wasn't a great man, he was, at least, a great
poster.
Margot Asquith

Democracy is four wolves and a lamb, voting on what
to have for lunch.
Wilma Brown

We women politicians have all the men out there
worrying that we'll all have PMS on the same day and
blow up the town.
Barbara Carr

Most Conservatives believe that a crèche is something
that happens between two Range Rovers in Tunbridge
Wells.
Caroline Shorten

I always knew Lloyd George won the war, but until I
read his memoirs I didn't know he'd done it
single-handedly.
Margot Asquith

Calvin Coolidge looked as if he'd been weaned on a
pickle.   *Alice Roosevelt Longworth*

The idea of Prince Charles conversing with vegetables
isn't quite so surprising when you remember he's had
plenty of time chatting to members of his own family.
                                          Jaci Stephens

Theodore Roosevelt was an old maid with testosterone
poisoning.   *Patricia O'Toole*

George Bush's problem is that the clothes have no
emperor.   *Anna Quinlan*

Politicians are like nappies. They should be changed
often – and for the same reason.   *Maureen Potter*

Winston Churchill would kill his own mother just so
that he could use her skin to make a drum to beat his
own praises.   *Margot Asquith*

My husband always said that his acting life was good
preparation for politics.   *Nancy Reagan*

There's nothing in socialism that a little money won't
cure.   *Will Durant*

If politicians don't do it to their wives, they do it to
their country.   *Mel Brooks*

Anybody who wants the Presidency so much that he'll spend two years organising and campaigning for it is not to be trusted with the office.   *David Broder*

The Tory Party is the cream of England: rich, thick and full of clots.   *Graffiti*

The first requirement of a statesman is that he be dull.
Dean Acheson

There are three times in a man's life when it's useless to hold him to anything: when he's madly in love, drunk or running for office.   *Robert Mitchum*

Ask not what your country can do for you. Most of the politicians are corrupt anyway.   *Rita Coolidge*

The vote means nothing to women. We should be armed.   *Edna O'Brien*

If a man hasn't discovered something that he will die for, he isn't fit to live.   *Martin Luther King*

There's one thing about being president – nobody can tell you when to sit down.   *Dwight D Eisenhower*

I never vote for anybody. I always vote against.
W C Fields

I never dared to be radical when young for fear it would make me conservative when old.   *Robert Frost*

A government which robs Peter to pay Paul can always depend on the support of Paul.   *George Bernard Shaw*

Communism is like Prohibition. It's a good idea but it won't work.   *Will Rogers*

The cure for admiring the House of Lords is to go and look at it.   *Walter Bagehot*

The Welfare State should really be called the Farewell State.   *J B Priestley*

Politics is too serious to be left to the politicians.
Charles de Gaulle

The thing about a politician is, you have to take the smooth with the smooth.   *Susan Hill*

Ninety-eight per cent of the adults in America are decent, hard-working and honest. It's the other two per cent that get all the publicity. But then – we elected them.   *Lily Tomlin*

Nancy Reagan's skin is so tight, every time she crosses her legs, her mouth snaps open.   *Joan Rivers*

Communists all seem to wear small caps, a look I consider better suited to tubes of toothpaste than people.   *Fran Lebowitz*

I don't know a lot about politics, but I can recognise a good party man when I see one.   *Mae West*

It is well known that the most radical revolutionary
will become a conservative on the day after the
revolution.
                                            Hannah Arendt

Politicians, like the Chinese, all look alike.
                                            Veronica Lake

In politics women type the letters, lick the stamps,
distribute the pamphlets and get out the vote. Men get
elected.
                                            Claire Boothe Luce

Franklin Roosevelt was two-thirds mush and one-third
Eleanor.
                                    Alice Roosevelt Longworth

It's not a good idea for a woman to enter politics. It
takes too long to do two faces.
                                            Lily Tomlin

When Richard Nixon is alone in a room, is there
anyone there?
                                            Gloria Steinem

All government violence can do is breed
counter-violence.
                                            Nelson Mandela

It's not the voting that's democracy; it's the counting.
                                            Tom Stoppard

I'm a Communist by day and a Catholic as soon as it
gets dark.
                                            Brendan Behan

Politics is the second oldest profession on earth – and
it bears a gross resemblance to the first.
                                            Ronald Reagan

Liberals are just as fearful as reactionaries. For every 'Disgusted of Tunbridge Wells', there's a 'Horrified of Hampstead'.

Julie Birchill

If I had to choose between betraying my country and betraying my friend, I hope I should have the guts to betray my country.

E M Forster

There are two kinds of women: those who want power in the world and those who want power in bed.

Jacqueline Onassis

If you go into a campus these days, people are too busy reading *The Wall Street Journal* to protest.

Fionnuala Flanagan

Nationalism is an infantile disease, the measles of mankind.

Albert Einstein

Communists are people who fancied that they had an unhappy childhood.

Gertrude Stein

My only political ambition is to be re-elected.

Glenda Jackson

War has become a luxury that only small nations can afford.

Hannah Arendt

I don't mind how much my Ministers talk, as long as they do what I say in the end.

Margaret Thatcher

Margaret Thatcher was the best man in the Tory Party.
Barbara Castle

You can no more win a war than you can win an earthquake.
Jeanette Rankin

Revolution is the solution to pollution.
Peter Cagney

Free Northern Ireland. Just send six box tops and a self-addressed envelope.
Graffiti

The more you read about politics, you realise that one party is worse than the other.
Will Rogers

When you're abroad, you're a statesman. When you're at home you're just a politician.
Harold Macmillan

Politicians promise to build a bridge even where there's no river.
Nikita Khrushchev

There will be no whitewash at the White House.
Richard Nixon

Every successful revolution puts on in time the robes of the tyrant it has deposed.
Barbara Tuchman

It's a pity that more politicians are not bastards by birth rather than reputation.
Katharine Whitehorn

Practical politics consists in ignoring facts.
Henry Brooks Adams

When you're on the periphery it's not the periphery;
it's the centre. **Mary Robinson**

I don't make jokes. I just watch the government and
report the facts. **Will Rogers**

Do you realise the responsibility I carry? I'm the only
person standing between Nixon and the White House.
John F Kennedy

It was so cold last week, even the politicians were
walking round with their hands in their own pockets.
Bob Hope

In America any boy may become president. It's just
one of the risks he takes. **Adlai Stevenson**

I won't eat anything that has intelligent life, but I
would gladly eat a network executive or a politician.
Marty Feldman

Margaret Thatcher surprised everyone by buying a
house in Dulwich instead of moving to Bolivia with
the rest of the Nazis. **Jo Brand**

Patriots always talk of dying for their country but
never of killing for their country. **Bertrand Russell**

Reforms are less to be dreaded than revolutions, for
they cause less reaction. **Justice Darling**

Fleas can be taught nearly everything that a
Congressman can.

Mark Twain

George Washington said to his father, 'How can I get
to be president if I never tell a lie?'

Red Buttons

A politician is a person who approaches every situation
with an open mouth.

Adlai Stevenson

Not while I'm alive he ain't!

*Ernest Bevin in response to the allegation that Herbert
Morrison was his own worst enemy*

In politics, shared hatreds are almost always the basis of
friendships.

Alexis de Tocqueville

A politician is a person who will double-cross a bridge
before he comes to it.

Oscar Levant

I have learned that one of the most important rules of
politics is poise, which means looking like an owl after
you've behaved like a jackass.

Ronald Reagan

The best Government is a benevolent tyranny
tempered by an occasional assassination.

Voltaire

A despot easily forgives his subjects for not loving him,
provided they do not love each other.

Alexis de Tocqueville

A reactionary is a somnambulist walking backwards.

Franklin D Roosevelt

Revolution is a trivial shift in the emphasis of suffering.
Tom Stoppard

Republics show the art of running the circus from the monkey cage.
H L Mencken

Democracy is the worst form of government apart from all the other ones.
Winston Churchill

A politician is someone who believes you don't have to fool all the people all the time. Just during elections.
Stanley Davis

There's only one way to leave power, and that's kicking and screaming.
P J Mara

The typical socialist is a prim little man with a white collar job, usually a secret teetotaller and often with vegetarian leanings, with a history of nonconformity behind him – and above all, with a social position he has no intention of forfeiting. As with the Christian religion, the worst advertisement for socialism is its adherents.
George Orwell

I make a fortune from criticising the policy of the Government . . . and then hand it over to the Government in taxes to keep it going.
George Bernard Shaw

I never give the public hell. I just tell the truth, and they *think* it's hell.
Harry Truman

I don't feel I'll ever get credit for anything I do in Foreign Affairs no matter how successful it is, because I didn't go to Harvard.

Lyndon Baines Johnson

Democracy is the recurrent suspicion that more than half the people are right more than half the time.

E B White

I have this dream that someday my son will become President of the United States. He'll still be messing up my life, but at least he'll be getting paid for it.

Ryan O'Neal

The most distinctive characteristic of the successful politician is selective cowardice.

Richard Harris

A politician should have three hats: one for throwing in the ring, one for talking through, and one for pulling rabbits out of if elected.

Carl Sandberg

Joe McCarthy is the only major politician in America who can be labelled 'liar' without fear of libel.

Joseph Stewart Alsop

Eleanor Roosevelt got even with her enemies in a way that was almost cruel. She forgave them.

Ralph McGill

Socialism is nothing but the capitalism of the lower classes.

Oswald Spengler

Bill Clinton's foreign policy experience stems mainly from having had breakfast at the International House of Pancakes.

Pat Buchanan

It would be desirable if every government, when it comes into power, should have its old speeches burned.
Philip Snowden

Power corrupts, but lack of power corrupts absolutely.
Adlai Stevenson

An election is a moral horror, as bad as a battle except for the blood, a mudbath for every soul concerned in it.
George Bernard Shaw

Every time we find an answer to The Irish Question, the Irish change the question. *Winston Churchill*

He looked at foreign affairs through the wrong end of a municipal drainpipe.
Winston Churchill on Neville Chamberlain

How could they tell?
Dorothy Parker after hearing President Calvin Coolidge had died

The nine most terrifying words in the English language are: 'I'm from the government and I'm here to help'.
Ronald Reagan

Franco's funeral!
Brendan Behan after being asked what he would most like to see when he went to Spain

Al Gore is in danger of becoming all things to no people. *Paul Bogard*

I thought he was a young man of promise, but it
appears he was a young man of promises.
Arthur Balfour on Churchill

I've been married to a communist and a fascist, and
neither of them would take out the trash.   *Zsa Zsa Gabor*

The world would not be in such a snarl,
Had Marx been Groucho instead of Karl.   *Irving Berlin*

A woman voting for divorce is like a turkey voting for
Christmas.   *Alice Glenn*

Gladstone speaks to me as if I were a public meeting.
Queen Victoria

He knows nothing and thinks he knows everything.
That points clearly to a political career.
George Bernard Shaw

Calvin Coolidge didn't say much and when he did he
didn't say much.   *Will Rogers*

The most extraordinary collection of talent that has
ever been gathered together at the White House, with
the possible exception of when Thomas Jefferson dined
alone.
John F Kennedy to a collection of Nobel Prize Winners in 1962

A year ago Gerald Ford was unknown throughout
America. Now he's unknown throughout the world.
The Guardian, 1974

If the word 'no' was removed from the English
language, Ian Paisley would be struck speechless.
John Hume

The Eichmann trial taught the world the banality of
evil; Nixon taught it the evil of banality.   *Ivan Stone*

A pig-eyed bag of wind.   *Frank Howley on Khrushchev*

John Major is marginally better than cystitis.   *Jo Brand*

Being criticised by Geoffrey Howe is like being savaged
by a dead sheep.   *Denis Healey*

Those who make peaceful revolution impossible will
make violent revolution inevitable.   *John F Kennedy*

About one-fifth of the people are against everything all
the time.   *Robert Kennedy*

A diplomat these days is nothing but a head-waiter
who's allowed to sit down occasionally.   *Peter Ustinov*

I've been thinking of making a proposition to my
Republican friends: if they stop telling lies about the
Democrats, we'll stop telling the truth about them.
Adlai Stevenson

When you make your peace with authority, you
become authority.   *Jim Morrison*

They never miss an opportunity to miss an opportunity.   ***Conor Cruise O'Brien on Ulster Unionists***

The Treasury could not, with any degree of success, run a fish and chip shop.   ***Harold Wilson***

A demagogue is a person with whom we disagree as to which gang should mismanage the country.
Don Marquis

The most desirable qualification for a politician is the ability to foretell what is going to happen tomorrow, next week, next month and next year . . . and to have the ability afterwards to say why it didn't.
Winston Churchill

Democracy means government by the uneducated, while aristocracy means government by the badly educated.   ***G K Chesterton***

Man is born perfect; it is the capitalist system that corrupts him.   ***Arthur Scargill***

Sometimes I look at Billy and Jimmy and I say to myself, 'Lillian, you should have stayed a virgin.'
Lillian Carter

RELIGION

We never ask God to forgive anybody except where we haven't.   ***Elbert Hubbard***

It takes six simpletons and one zealot to start a movement.
Anzia Yezierska

There are Ten Commandments, but only six need to be attempted.
Hilaire Belloc

If you go to heaven without being naturally qualified for it, you will not enjoy yourself there.
George Bernard Shaw

Catholics sow their wild oats from Monday to Saturday and then go to Mass on Sunday praying for a crop failure.
Tommy Makem

God may be dead, but 50,000 social workers have risen to take His place.
John McCaughey

Use Moses' cure for constipation: take two tablets and go up the mountain.
Larry McCabe

Church bazaars are fêtes worse than death.
Robert Morley

The church complains of persecution when it is not allowed to persecute.
Luis de Zulusta

An atheist is a man with no invisible means of support.
John Buchan

In the 19th century, the problem was that God was dead. In the 20th century, the problem is that *man* is dead. In the 19th century, inhumanity meant cruelty; in the 20th century it means schizoid self-alienation. The danger of the past was that men became slaves; the danger of the future is that men may become robots.

Erich Fromm

It is the final proof of God's omnipotence that He need not exist in order to save us.   **Peter de Vries**

There are no atheists in the foxholes.

William Thomas Cummings

I do benefits for all religions. I don't want to blow the hereafter on a technicality.   **Bob Hope**

A logarithm is a Catholic birth control record.

John Crosbie

We should live our lives as though Christ were coming this afternoon.   **Jimmy Carter**

If only God would give us some clear sign. Like making a large deposit in my name at a Swiss bank.

Woody Allen

God is a living doll.   **Jane Russell**

All great truths begin as blasphemies.

George Bernard Shaw

The highest praise of God consists in the denial of Him by the atheist, who finds creation so perfect it can dispense with a creator. *Marcel Proust*

Millions long for eternity who wouldn't know what to do with themselves on a rainy Sunday afternoon. *Susan Ertz*

Three wise men? You must be joking. *Rita Rudner*

God and I have a great relationship, but we both see other people. *Dolly Parton*

I think that God in creating man, somewhat overestimated his ability. *Oscar Wilde*

I used to be in favour of women priests, but two years in the Cabinet cured me of that. *Norman St John-Stevas*

When I started out, people were afraid of parish priests. Now they're afraid of newspaper editors. *Michael D Higgins*

God to me is a verb, not a noun. *Roger Fry*

We have grasped the mystery of the atom and rejected the Sermon On The Mount. *Omar Bradley*

Better an authentic Mammon than a bogus god. *Louis McNeice*

I am prepared to meet my Maker. Whether my Maker is prepared for the great ordeal of meeting me is quite another matter. **Winston Churchill**

God doesn't play dice with the universe. **Albert Einstein**

Nothing makes one so vain as being told that one is a sinner. **Oscar Wilde**

In the frontlines of Korea I never saw a pin-up of an actress, but I saw hundreds of Bibles. **Billy Graham**

The future is like heaven: everyone exalts it, but nobody wants to go there. **Anon**

Don't become an atheist. There aren't enough holidays. **Mort Sahl**

The Bible is a prophet and lust account. **Colin Bowles**

The orgasm has replaced the cross as the focus of longing and the image of fulfilment. **Malcolm Muggeridge**

One of the thieves was saved. It's a reasonable percentage. **Samuel Beckett**

Going to Limerick and not having a drink is like going to church and not saying a prayer. **Richard Harris**

To put one's trust in God is only a longer way of saying that one will chance it. **Samuel Butler**

As for the British clergyman, he goes to church as he goes to the bathroom, with the minimum of fuss and with no explanation if he can help it.   *Ronald Blythe*

If Jeffrey Archer is going to heaven, I'd prefer to go to Lewisham.   *Spike Milligan shortly before he died*

Often it seems a pity Noah and his party didn't miss the boat.   *Mark Twain*

There's a pretty strong case against God for cruelty to animals.   *Henry Cecil*

When Jesus called Peter from his boat He spoiled an honest man.   *George Bernard Shaw*

If God had to give women wrinkles, He might at least have put them on the soles of their feet.   *Ninon de Lenclos*

There's only one difference between Catholics and Jews. Jews are born with guilt whereas Catholics have to go to school to learn it.   *Elayne Boosler*

Why is it that when we talk to God we're said to be praying, but when God talks to us, we're schizophrenic?   *Lily Tomlin*

God gives us our relatives – thank God we can choose our friends.   *Ethel Watts Mumford*

The Lord said, 'Let there be wheat', and Saskatchewan was born.
Stephen Leacock

We should take care not to make the intellect our god. It has powerful muscles, but no personality.
Albert Einstein

Giving away a fortune is taking Christianity too far.
Charlotte Bingham

If man is only a little lower than the angels, it makes you wonder about the angels.
Bertrand Russell

Men don't get cellulite, which confirms my belief that God is, after all, male.
Rita Rudner

I respect faith, but doubt is what gets you an education.
Wilson Mizner

Jesus would be framed and in jail if he was living today.
Carson McCullers

Psychology is the theology of the 20th century.
Harry Norton

Religions tend to disappear with men's good fortune.
Raymond Queneau

Never take a reference from a clergyman: they always want to give someone a second chance.
Arnold Bennett

We are in the world to laugh. In purgatory we shall no longer be able to do so, and in heaven it would not be proper.

Jules Renard

Televangelists are ecumenical with the truth.

John Crosbie

The more ridiculous a belief system, the higher the probability of its success.

Wayne Barta

Whom the gods wish to destroy, they first call promising.

Cyril Connolly

The resurrection of the body, unless much improved in construction, would be a terrible mistake.

Evelyn Underhill

Every man thinks God is on his side. The rich and powerful know he is.

Jean Anouilh

Beware of the man whose God is in the skies.

George Bernard Shaw

Is man one of God's blunders? Or is God one of man's blunders?

Friedrich Nietzsche

If God had meant us to be gay, he would have put Adam and Steve in the Garden of Eden.

Graffiti

I believe in the eucharist of the nothingness of life.

Paul Durcan

Christ died for our sins. Dare we make his martyrdom meaningless by not committing them?   *Jules Pfeiffer*

I don't want to go to heaven if I have to stand all the time.   *Spike Milligan*

Men will wrangle for religion, write for it, fight for it and die for it – anything but live for it.   *Charles Colton*

The Lord prefers common-looking people. That's why he makes so many of them.   *Abraham Lincoln*

If God didn't want man to hunt, he wouldn't have given us plaid shirts.   *Johnny Carson*

I didn't believe in reincarnation the last time either.
   Graffiti

A heretic is someone who disagrees with you on something neither of you know anything about.
   H L Mencken

Every reformation must have its victims. You can't expect the fatted calf to share the enthusiasm of the angels over the prodigal's return.   *Saki*

If it has to choose who is to be crucified, the crowd will always save Barabbas.   *Jean Cocteau*

You have to be very religious to change your religion.
   Comtesse Diane

The family that prays together stays together. Thank God my father's an agnostic. **Sid James**

The major sin is the sin of being born. **Samuel Beckett**

Christmas Day is the feast of Saint Loneliness. **Paul Durcan**

God must have been a Protestant. He only had one son. **Colin Wilson**

Many people feel they're attracted to God when they're merely repelled by man. **W R Inge**

Catholics commit more sins than any other religion, but get less fun out of it. **Woody Allen**

The trouble with born-again Christians is that they're an even bigger pain the second time around. **Herb Caen**

Jesus saves, but then he's not on PAYE. **Graffiti**

If God was condemned to live the life he has inflicted on others, he would kill himself. **Alexandre Dumas**

Saints should be judged guilty until proven innocent. **George Orwell**

Reincarnation is just a sneaky way to sell more tombstones. **Robert Orpen**

It is so stupid of modern civilisation to have given up believing in the devil when he is the only explanation of it.
Ronald Knox

If triangles invented a God, they'd make him 3-sided.
Baron de Montesquieu

Apart from theology and sex there's really nothing to talk about.
Harold Laski

Women give themselves to God when the devil wants no more to do with them.
Sophie Arnould

Gods make their own importance.
Patrick Kavanagh

I wouldn't take the Pope too seriously. He's a Pole first, a Pope second, and maybe a Christian third.
Muriel Spark of Pope John Paul II

It angers me to see Rangers or Celtic fanatics getting all steamed up in the name of religion when most of them have never been near a church in years.
Derek Johnstone

Saints have died out from sheer inability to propagate their species.
Norman Douglas

Oysters are more beautiful than any religion . . . There's nothing in Christianity or Buddhism that quite matches the sympathetic unselfishness of an oyster.
Saki

Perhaps God is not dead, but mad.
R D Laing

Scratch a Christian and you'll find a pagan.

Israel Zangwill

Roman Catholics have shaken off the nightmare of monotheism. Their Trinity is broken up, the Holy Ghost having evaporated in the course of years, as spirits often do.

Norman Douglas

Those who marry God can become domesticated too. It's just as humdrum a marriage as all the others.

Graham Greene

Heaven for the climate, hell for the company.

J M Barrie

Poor Matthew Arnold, he's gone to heaven, no doubt. But he won't like God.

Robert Louis Stevenson

I only want to go to heaven if Hank Williams is there.

Billy Connolly

I don't suppose angels have any sense of humour; you see it would be no use to them as they never hear any jokes.

Saki

Man created God in his image.

Bertrand Russell

It is the test of a good religion whether you can make a joke about it.

G K Chesterton

If there's no God, who opens the door in supermarkets?

Patrick Murray

Saints are all right in heaven, but they're hell on earth.
Cardinal Cushing

To the lexicographer, God is simply the word that comes next to go-cart. **Samuel Butler**

She was an atheist and I was an agnostic. We didn't know what religion *not* to bring our children up in.
Woody Allen

I read the book of Job last night. I don't think God comes well out of it. **Virginia Woolf**

My husband and I divorced over religious differences. He thought he was God and I didn't. **Joan Rivers**

The trouble with God is that he thinks he's Bono.
Michael Brophy

Malcolm Muggeridge thinks he was knocked off his horse by God, like St Paul on the road to Damascus. His critics think he simply fell off from old age.
Katharine Whitehorn

The Catholic Church has never really come to terms with women. What I object to is being treated either as Madonnas or Mary Magdalenes. **Shirley Williams**

I've looked on a lot of women with lust. I've committed adultery in my heart many times. This is something God recognises I will do and forgives me for it. **Jimmy Carter**

SELF-CRITICISM

I got thrown out of Alcoholics Anonymous because when the other guys saw me, they thought they were having the DTs.
Dave Dutton

The absurd thing about being a duke or a prince is that you are a professional ignoramus.
Duke of Gloucester

I never go to other people's funerals. They won't go to mine.
Bob Monkhouse

I'm ageing about as well as a beach party movie.
Harvey Fierstein

My face looks like a wedding cake that has been left out in the rain.
W H Auden

If only I had known, I would have become a watchmaker.
Albert Einstein after his splitting of the atom gave rise to the atom bomb

Descriptions of my face have included comparisons with most root vegetables.
Frankie Howerd

Academia and various power groups only consider me a drunken slob and they're right there except I sometimes do things better sloshed than they do sober, staid and sinless.
Charles Bukowski

One year *The Harvard Lampoon* voted me the worst actor of the year, an honour I had truly earned. I was to acting what Laurence Olivier was to pop music.

Eddie Fisher

I have flabby thighs, but fortunately my stomach covers them.

Dawn French

I may be fat, but I'm thin inside. Has it ever struck you that there's a thin man inside every fat man just as they say there's a statue inside every block of stone?

George Orwell

I am always a perfectly safe man to tell any dirt to as it goes in one ear and out of my mouth.

Ernest Hemingway

I am not a gentleman. Someone once said gentlemen come into rooms. Harris prefers to make an entrance.

Richard Harris

I'm not a philosopher. Guilty bystander, that's my role.

Peter O'Toole

Tales of my toughness are exaggerated. I never killed an actor, for instance.

John Huston

I have gangster tendencies. I'd like to do the perfect bank robbery. I learned the facts of life from lavatory walls and dirty books.

Fr Michael Cleary

Deep down I'm rather shallow.

Charles Haughey

Don't tell my mother I work in an advertising agency.
She thinks I play piano in a brothel.   *Jacques Seguela*

I have done for rugby what Quasimodo did for
coat-hangers.   *Tom McNab*

I told my psychiatrist that everyone hates me. He said
I was being ridiculous – everyone hasn't met me yet.
                                       Rodney Dangerfield

I'm an uncultured, polo-playing clot.   *Prince Philip*

My mother was from the Caribbean, so I'm a one-eyed
Puerto Rican Jewish nigger who happens to be married
to a white woman. When I move into a new
neighbourhood people run in four different directions
at the same time.   *Sammy Davis Jr*

Seeing ourselves as others see us would probably
confirm our worst suspicions about them.
                                        Franklin P Jones

I'd rather be called sleazy than identified as intelligent.
                                           Phil Donahoe

I can resist everything except temptation.   *Oscar Wilde*

If the fence is strong enough I'll sit on it.   *Sir Cyril Smith*

I don't dig ballet. The last time I went to one, my
friends bet a lot of money on the swan to live.
                                            Woody Allen

I'm a severe critic. If a person has a hole in their sock, they crumble before me.

Morrissey

When I discovered I had no talent or vocation for any job, I joined the Civil Service.

Moss Keane

At least I have the modesty to admit that lack of modesty is one of my failings.

Hector Berlioz

I've done commercials in Australia I'd pay not to see.

John Cleese

Someone cruelly pointed out in print that I looked like an unmade bed.

Dylan Thomas

I'm so bad I make medicine sick.

Muhammad Ali

Actors think they make a film and think they're curing cancer. To hell with that. We serve less purpose to the community than a garbage collector.

James Caan

I made a lot of movies early in my career in the hope that I would become a star before people realised I couldn't act.

Michael Caine

Be careful, sport, that is libel of the very worst kind.

Errol Flynn to a journalist who said he was going to write a story suggesting Flynn had finally stopped drinking

I have a Split personality.

A punning Goran Ivanisevic – he comes from Split, Croatia – succinctly describes his schizophrenic nature after winning Wimbledon in 2001

I look like a cross between my father, Mephistopheles and an opium peddler on the Mexican border.

Groucho Marx

I took to freebasing cocaine. One hit of that and I said, 'What job? What wife? Are you kidding me?'

Tony Curtis

I drink to destroy myself.

Jack Kerouac

I am being frank about myself in this book. I tell of my first mistake on page 850.

Henry Kissinger on his autobiography

I was so ugly when I was born, the doctor slapped my mother.

Henny Youngman

I have always disliked myself at any given moment. The total of such moments is my life.

Cyril Connolly

I am to cricket what Dame Sybil Thorndike is to non-ferrous welding.

Frank Muir

I started at the top and worked my way down.

Orson Welles

Right now I'm moving through my personal life like a haemophiliac in a razor factory.

Robin Williams in 1988

There are two kinds of egotists: those who admit it, and the rest of us.

Laurence J Peter

The main reason for my success? My pretensions
became popular.   *Paul Simon*

More and more these days I find myself pondering
how to reconcile my gross habits with my net income.
                                                   Kirk Nelson

You have no idea what a poor opinion I have of myself
– and how little I deserve it.   *W S Gilbert*

I write for myself and strangers. The strangers, dear
readers, are an afterthought.   *Gertrude Stein*

The American public wants a solemn ass for president,
and I think I'll go along with them.   *Calvin Coolidge*

Of every four words I write, I strike out three.
                                                   Niels Bohr

My mother didn't like me. She'd say, 'Remember when
you're crossing the road, look up, look down, look up,
look down . . .'   *Joan Rivers*

I don't deserve this. But I have arthritis and I don't
deserve that either.   *Jack Benny after receiving an award*

They once showed a video of me playing snooker to
try and bring a man out of a coma in hospital. It
worked. After ten minutes he struggled out of the bed
to turn off the tape.   *Steve Davis*

I was the first child in my family to own a Cadillac, the first to have a formal wedding and the first to fly to Europe. And I'm the last one to ever admit I'm wrong.
Chuck Berry

When I was 14 I asked my dad to buy me a model railway instead of a guitar. What I do now is all his fault.
Rod Stewart

I'm not from the working class. I'm from the criminal class.
Peter O'Toole

I may not have been a good Prime Minister, but I would have been a brilliant farmer.
Golda Meir

I used to think I was an interesting person until I got to page 35 of my autobiography and realised I had nothing else to say.
Roseanne Arnold

I have no self-confidence. When girls say yes to me, I tell them to go home and think it over.
Rodney Dangerfield

At my age I refuse to wear a beeper. I don't want anything else on my body that might fall off.
George Burns

I have two basic problems. I think everybody else is better than me – and so do they.
Louis Safian

I never drink unless I'm alone or with someone.
W C Fields

As a writer, I'm nothing more than a perfect sausage machine. *Agatha Christie*

When I told people I was going to be a comedian they laughed. But they're not laughing now. *Bob Hope*

I got to Hollywood on a Monday and was fired by Wednesday. The guy that hired me was out of town on Tuesday. *Raymond Chandler on his screenwriting career*

There was a time when I thought my only connection with the literary world would be that I once delivered meat to T S Eliot's mother-in-law. *Alan Bennett*

I'm just as good a mother as the next repressed, obsessive-compulsive paranoiac. *Anne Lamott*

Write to amuse? What an appalling suggestion! I write to make people anxious and miserable and to worsen their indigestion. *Wendy Cope*

I'm at the age where just putting my cigar into the holder is a thrill. *George Burns at 87*

My computer dating programme came up with a perfect gentleman. Still, I've got another three goes. *Sally Poplin*

The first thing I always look for in a script is days off. *Spencer Tracy*

I'm overdrawn at the bank. I won't say by how much, but if you saw it written down you'd think it was a sex chatline telephone number.   *Julie Birchill*

I'm not indecisive. Am I indecisive?
Jim Scheibel, former Mayor of St Paul

I am always ready to learn although I do not always like being taught.   *Winston Churchill*

I left school at fifteen having passed just one test: my cervical smear one.   *Kathy Lette*

Some of my jokes would make rhubarb grow.
Roy 'Chubby' Brown

I got an antique watch from my grandfather on his deathbed. It wasn't easy – he put up a hell of a fight for it.   *Woody Allen*

I see nothing wrong with power as long as I'm the fellow who has it.   *Cecil King*

I only know two tunes. One of them is *Yankee Doodle* and the other isn't.   *Ulysses S Grant*

Every time I paint a portrait I lose a friend.
John Singer Sargent

I won't say ours was a tough school, but we had our own coroner. We used to write essays like, 'What I'm going to be if I grow up.'   *Lenny Bruce*

They say a man is as old as the woman he feels. In that case, I'm 85.

Groucho Marx

Man's dilemma is that we hate change and love it at the same time. What we really want is for things to remain the same but get better.

Sydney Harris

I bring out the worst in my enemies. That's how I get them to defeat themselves.

Roy Cohn

I do unto others what they do unto me, only worse.

Jimmy Hoffa

I'm very balanced. I'm an exhibitionist, but also a voyeur.

Woody Harrelson

I love to smoke so much I'm gonna get a tracheotomy so I can have two cigarettes at the same time.

Denis Leary

My town is so boring, anyone who stays up to watch the 11 o'clock news is classed as a playboy.

Fred Allen

I never mistreated a girl in my life – except for the ones I married. You have to pay for that privilege.

James Caan

I got my start in silent radio.

Bob Monkhouse

I'm not saying my body is bad, but my gynaecologist wears a hard hat.

Joan Rivers

I drink too much. The last time I gave a urine sample it had an olive in it. **Rodney Dangerfield**

During my footballing days I used to go missing a lot. Miss Canada, Miss United Kingdom, Miss Germany. **George Best**

Anorexics look in the mirror and see somebody fat. Therefore I'm anorexic. **Dawn French**

THE ANIMAL WORLD

They told me it takes three sheep to make a cardigan. I didn't even know they could knit. **Sue Gingold**

One day when I was in the jungle I shot an elephant in my pyjamas. What he was doing in my pyjamas I'll never know. **Groucho Marx**

Man is a dog's ideal of what God should be. **Holbrook Jackson**

Mr Cat knows that a whisker spied is not a whole mouse. **Marguerite Henry**

I have just been given a very engaging Persian kitten, and his opinion is that I have been given to *him*. **Evelyn Underhill**

It would make good sense to cross a homing pigeon with a parrot. If it got lost, it could ask the way home. **Penelope Taylor**

Did you hear about the parrot who went cheap? They forgot to send the bill. **Kenny Everett**

I watched a herd of elephants travelling through dense forest – pacing along as if they had an appointment at the end of the world. **Isak Dinesen**

We don't own our dogs. Our dogs own us. **Dodie Smith**

Dogs are wise. They crawl away into a quiet corner and lick their wounds and do not rejoin the world until they are whole once more. **Agatha Christie**

What would you get if you crossed a sheep with a kangaroo? A woolly jumper. **Des Bishop**

Customer in pet shop: Have you any dogs going cheap?
Owner: No, all our dogs go 'woof'. **Nigel Rees**

The reason cats learned to see in the dark is because they're too short to reach the light switch. **Caroline Lewis**

I once brought a pig into my house. I was worried about the smell but it didn't prove to be a problem. After a while he got used to it. **Quentin Crisp**

I'm all for guns. I think we should give them to everybody. Especially ducks. How can you call hunting a sport when only one side has a chance of winning? **Elaine Boosler**

Grandmother once took her umbrella to a man who was beating a horse. When she was through with him, he was glad to be turned over to the police.   *Ilka Chase*

Orang-utans teach us that looks aren't everything.
Will Cuppy

Beasts kill for hunger, men for pay.   *John Gay*

Man is the only animal that blushes – or needs to.
Mark Twain

To confess that you are totally ignorant about the horse is social suicide. You will be despised by everyone, especially the horse.   *W C Sellar*

There are two things for which animals are to be envied. They know nothing of future evils, or of what people say of them.   *Voltaire*

At the annual sheepdog trials, how many sheep were found guilty?   *Graffiti*

I find that ducks' opinions of me are greatly influenced by whether or not I have bread.   *Mitch Hedberg*

Two kangaroos were talking to each other and one says, 'Gee, I hope it doesn't rain today. I hate it when the children play inside.'   *Henny Youngman*

A cat is a soft indestructible automaton provided by nature to be kicked when things go wrong in the domestic circle.   *Ambrose Bierce*

We've got a cat called Ben Hur. We called it Ben till it had kittens.
Sally Poplin

Imagine if birds were tickled by feathers. You'd see a whole flock of them coming by, laughing hysterically.
Steven Wright

If you weighed all the earthworms in the United States, they would be something like 55 times heavier than the combined weight of all Americans.
Geoff Tibballs

Men are those creatures with two legs and eight hands.
Jayne Mansfield

The Smithsonian Museum found my wife's shoe. On the basis of its measurements they constructed a dinosaur.
Woody Allen

When a dog is drowning, everyone offers him water.
Proverb

Don't make the mistake of treating dogs like humans or they'll treat you like dogs.
Martha Scott

If Darwin was right, my dog would have learned to operate the can-opener by now.
Ricky Gervais

Scientists think they can now clone an all-white zebra. Now I'm no expert, but isn't that a horse?
Jay Leno

Van Gogh would have sold more than one painting if he'd put tigers in them.
Tom Hobbes

If you think you have influence, try ordering someone else's dog around. **Josh Billings**

It is not the ape nor the tiger in man that I fear, but the donkey. **William Temple**

A dog in the home is a piece of moving furniture. **Philippe de Rothschild**

Hunting is 90% of the fun of war for 10% of the risk. **Philip Lee**

I'm much more comfortable being around gorillas than people. **Dian Fossey**

The bluebird carries the sky on his back. **Henry David Thoreau**

I never saw a wild thing sorry for itself. **D H Lawrence**

I was such an ugly kid, when I played in the sandbox, the cat kept covering me up. **Rodney Dangerfield**

History is more full of the fidelity of dogs than people. **Alexander Pope**

The lion and the calf shall lie down together, but the calf won't get much sleep. **Woody Allen**

Many people have equated the intelligence of the dolphin with that of man. I'm afraid that, in the comparison, the dolphin comes off rather badly. **Richard Harrison**

When the eagles are silent, the parrots begin to jabber.
Winston Churchill

We think of the dinosaur as a byword for something past its sell-by date, but they lasted 165 million years. I hope we are that successful.
Douglas Adams

You gotta get up early in the morning to catch a fox, and stay up late at night to get a mink.
Mae West

When you have an elephant by the hind leg and he's trying to run away, it's usually best to let him.
Alexander Lincoln

I'll never forget my youth. I was a teacher's pet. She couldn't afford a dog.
Rodney Dangerfield

TURNS OF PHRASE

Only the young die good.
Oliver Herford

A secret may sometimes be best kept by keeping the secret of it being a secret.
Sir Henry Taylor

One good turn and you have most of the bed covers.
Elaine Moore

A shotgun wedding is a matter of wife or death.
Peter Cagney

Don't trust your first impulses – they're always good.
Talleyrand

He who hesitates is bossed.   *Sonia Chapman*

More waist, less speed.   *David Walters*

A fat wife is a bird in a girdled cage.   *Jerry Lewis*

If you want to dress to please your husband, wear last
year's clothes.   *Joey Bishop*

Gather ye autographs while ye may.   *Cole Porter*

When the gods wish to punish us, they answer our
prayers.   *Oscar Wilde*

Many are cold, but few are frozen.   *Frank Muir*

If you want to make an omelette, you have to turn on
the microwave.   *Barbara Carson*

Familiarity breeds contempt – and some wonderful
quotations.   *John Charlton*

Don't drink on an empty head.   *Frank Skinner*

Love may make the world go round, but not as fast as
whiskey.   *Richard Harris*

You can fool too many people too much of the time.
                                           James Turber

The future ain't what it used to be.   *Yogi Berra*

People who live in glass houses have to answer the bell.
Bruce Patterson

He who laughs, lasts. *Mary Pettibone Poole*

Now is the winter of our discontent made glorious
summer by central heating. *Jack Sharkey*

Laugh and the world laughs with you, cry and you
have to blow your nose. *Doug Platt*

People who live in glass jaws shouldn't throw punches.
Jim Murray

A zebra cannot change its spots. *Dan Quayle*

In politics, where there's death there's hope.
Harold Laski

If it looks like a duck, walks like a duck and talks like
a duck it probably needs a little more time in the
microwave. *Lori Dowdy*

Laughter is the best medicine. Unless you've got VD,
in which case penicillin's probably a better bet.
Bob Monkhouse

Dada wouldn't buy me a Bauhaus. *Joan Sloan*

War hath no fury like a non-combatant. *C E Montague*

God said, 'Let there be light,' and there was, but the Electricity Board said he'd have to wait until Thursday to be connected. *Spike Milligan*

Curiosity killed the cat, but for a while I was a suspect. *Emo Philips*

Never change diapers in mid-stream. *Don Marquis*

Parking is such sweet sorrow. *Herb Caen*

Women – can't live with them, can't bury them in the backyard without the neighbours seeing. *Sean Williams*

Sticks and stones may break my bones but whips turn me on. *Gore Vidal*

An apple a day keeps the doctor away. An onion a day keeps everyone away. *Graffiti*

French dockers rule *au quai*. *Colin Jarman*

Eat, drink and be merry: tomorrow we may be radioactive. *Graffiti*

An Irish atheist is a man who wishes to God he could believe in God. *Graffiti*

Don't lose your nerve
About a curve
That oughter
Be shorter. *Tina Spencer Knott*

Invention is the mother of necessity. *Thorstein Veblen*

Many Hans make Volkswagens. *Graffiti*

Today it's politically incorrect to have close encounters with the furred kind. *Anon*

Uneasy is the head that wears the curlers. *Bette Midler*

Love your neighbour, but don't get caught. *Graffiti*

If the shoe fits, buy it in every available colour.
Imelda Marcos

If you can keep your head when all about you are losing theirs, you probably don't understand the problem. *Jean Kerr*

Two can live as cheaply as one . . . for half as long.
Howard Kandel

If you can't stand the heat, stay in the kitchen but move closer to the fridge. *Bill Cosby*

Nothing succeeds like failure. *Oliver Herford*

Will you take this woman to be your awful wedded wife? *Dylan Thomas*

Hell hath no fury like a woman's corns.
Leonard Levinson

An apology is the only thing that will enable you to have the last word with a woman. *Peter Cagney*

Many hands make light work, so put them all up to the bulb in the event of a power failure. *Michael Sheridan*

The hand that rocks the cradle is usually attached to someone who isn't getting enough sleep. *Jim Fiebig*

There's nothing like a Great Dane. *Angela Mitchell*

When your boat finally does come in, it's often the *Titanic*. *Trevor Griffiths*

The verb 'To diet' can only be conjugated in the future tense. *John Candy*

Money may not be able to buy happiness, but then happiness can't buy money either. *Henny Youngman*

Don't worry about the menopause – worry about the men who don't. *Joan Rivers*

People who live in glass houses shouldn't walk around naked. *Rita Rudner*

Too many cooks spoil the figure. *Phyllis Diller*

What shall it profit a man if he gains the whole world, and then there's a recession? *Mel Brooks*

Nero fiddled, but Coolidge only snored.
H L Mencken on Calvin Coolidge

Never hit anyone below the belt, particularly a black
one earned in karate.   *P J O'Rourke*

Men shall not live by bread alone, but too much butter
causeth cholesterol.   *Ralph Gleeson*

If at first you don't succeed, try a little ardour.
Nigel Rees

Never make a promise you can't break.   *Gene Kerrigan*

There but for the grace of God goes God.
Winston Churchill on Sir Stafford Cripps

People who love in glass houses should breathe on the
windows.   *P G Wodehouse*

Less is less.   *Martina Devlin*

There's no fool like a learned fool.   *Frank Sheed*

I would prefer to have a bottle in front of me than a
frontal lobotomy.   *Tom Waits*

Anything worth doing is worth doing badly.
G K Chesterton

Live and let die.   *Ian Fleming*

Dead men tell no tales. Posthumous fame is an Irish myth. *Israel Zangwill*

No good deed goes unpunished. *Oscar Wilde*

Justice must not only be seen to be done but seen to be believed. *J B Morton*

Man is born free but everywhere is in cellular underwear. *Jonathan Miller*

If at first you don't succeed, you're fired. *Jean Graman*

Start a movement: eat a prune. *Erma Bombeck*

East is east and west is San Francisco. *O Henry*

They've put a man on the moon. Now let's get the rest of them up there. *Kathy Lette*

To speed is human, to get caught a fine. *Colin Crampton*

Familiarity breeds. *Leonard Levinson*

Faith can move mountains. However, she's promised me she's going on a diet next week. *Sid Caesar*

Avoid clichés like the plague. *Arthur Christiansen*

Nothing succeeds like reputation. *John Huston*

There's no place like home – after the pubs close.
Brendan Behan

A boy's best friend is his mutter.
Michael Noonan

A friend that isn't in need is a friend indeed.
Kim Hubbard

You live and learn – and then you die and forget it all.
Noel Coward

Cleanliness may be next to godliness, but slobs make easier geniuses.
Philip Weir

Some men treat all women as sequels.
Anon

Women's Lib was a lot of dame foolishness.
Colin Crosbie

Cleanliness is next to the gas station.
Leonard Levinson

Yea, though I walk in the valley of death I shall fear no evil. I just think to myself: this place definitely wasn't named by a real estate developer.
Doug Finney

It is now proved beyond doubt that cigarettes are the greatest known cause of statistics.
Fletcher Knebel

Epigrams succeed where epics fail.
Persian proverb

Cleanliness is next to impossible.
Fran Lebowitz

Blessed are the young, for they shall inherit the national debt.   *Herbert Hoover*

Work is much more fun than fun.   *Noel Coward*

Since we have to speak well of the dead, let's knock 'em while they're alive.   *John Sloan*

You can't teach an old dogma new tricks.   *Dorothy Parker*

Actions lie louder than words.   *Carolyn Wells*

A woman's smile is like a bath tap. Turn it on and you find yourself in hot water.   *P G Wodehouse*

To err is human, but to really foul things up requires a computer.   *Anon*

A rose by any other name would be just as expensive.
Spike Milligan

WORK & BUSINESS

The meek may inherit the earth – but they'll never increase market share.   *William McGowan*

Secretaries will never go to heaven. We spend too much of our time telling little white lies.   *Gwen Cowan*

No one ever dies of hard work – but a lot of people die once they retire from it.   *Sir Ian McGregor*

Consumers know perfectly well that advertisements are biased. They expect them to be so. It's not dishonesty: it's a fair game that the consumer demands.   *Sir Tim Bell*

Sometimes I think the Civil Service suffers from a terrible disease. It's called the NIH which means 'not invented here'. In other words, anything they don't think up, they don't like.   *Freddie Laker*

I get a tremendous charge out of my work – the same sort of feeling women must have when their babies pop out.   *Terence Conran*

Start restructuring when things are going well and not when the water is already up to your neck.   *Fritz Leutwiler*

As well as a good academic record, I look for people who've climbed mountains or been captain of the tiddleywinks team at university. People other people will follow.   *John Banham*

It is the inescapable duty of management to fire incompetent people. This duty is often shirked. When you have to fire, have the guts to get on with it. You will be surprised how often the victim is relieved.   *David Ogilvy*

I don't meet competition: I crush it.
   Charles Revson, the founder of Revlon cosmetics

If I was given the choice of sweeping the floor or no work at all, I'd say, 'Pass me the goddam broom.'
Graham Day

As an airline boss I can travel first class and free on other airlines, but, frankly, I don't think I'd have the courage to ring them up and ask.   *Richard Branson*

You never have mergers without pain and a lot of dogs sniffing around at the bottom of the lamp-post.
Lord Reith

You don't get any marks for trying. I'm not interested in sophisticated reasons for failure.   *Sir Allen Sheppard*

There are too many one-ulcer men holding down two-ulcer jobs.   *Prince Charles*

The reason worry kills more people than work is because more people worry than work.   *Robert Frost*

The entrepreneur is like an eagle: he soars alone, he flies alone, he hunts alone.   *Dr Michael Smurfit*

Three characteristics of top executives are slow speech, impressive appearance . . . and a complete lack of a sense of humour.   *Johnson O'Connor*

When you lose your job it's a depression, when someone else loses theirs it's a *recession*.   *Jenny Eclair*

One cannot walk through a mass production factory and not feel that one is in hell. *W H Auden*

Nothing is more humiliating than to see idiots succeed in enterprises that we have failed in. *Gustave Flaubert*

Success and failure are both hard to endure. With success comes divorce, drugs, fornication, bullying, travel, meditation, medication, depression, neurosis and suicide. With failure comes failure. *Joseph Heller*

Commercialism is doing well that which should not be done at all. *Gore Vidal*

The ideal of the employer is to have products without employees; the ideal of the employee is to have income without work. *E F Schumacher*

There's nothing worse for a young man than to know he's rich enough to retire at 25. It held me back a lot. *Oliver Jessel*

In a hierarchy, every employee tends to rise to the level of his incompetence. *Dr Laurence J Peter*

If hard work were such a wonderful thing, surely the rich would have kept it all for themselves. *Lane Kirkland*

If you want something done, give it to a busy man . . . and he'll have his secretary do it. *Anon*

Luck isn't something you can mention in the presence of self-made men. *Elwyn Brooks White*

Consensus is when we have a discussion. They tell me what they think and then I decide. *Lee Iacocca*

Leaders must be seen to be upfront, up-to-date, up to their job . . . and up early in the morning. *Lord Sieff*

If you're not fired with enthusiasm you'll be fired with enthusiasm. *J Paul Getty*

Teamwork is always essential in a sales force. That way you always have someone to blame. *Donald Trump*

Success didn't spoil me. I've always been insufferable. *Fran Lebowitz*

Business is Darwinism: only the fittest survive. *Robert Holmes*

Like sex in Victorian England, the reality of big business today is our big dirty secret. *Ralph Nader*

Success has killed more men than bullets. *Texas Guinan*

Doing business without advertising is like winking at a girl in the dark. *You* know what you're doing, but nobody else does. *Edgar Howe*

A big shot is a little shot who kept shooting. *Louis Safian*

Accountancy is the closest to hell I've ever been.
Chris Blackwell

Advertising is the rattling of a stick inside a swill
bucket.
George Orwell

The real problem is not whether machines think but
whether men do.
Frederic Skinner

Good bankers, like good tea, can only be appreciated
when they're in hot water.
Jaffar Hussein

Few people do business well who do nothing else.
Lord Chesterfield

A camel looks like a horse that was designed by a
committee.
Anon

Meetings are rather like cocktail parties. You don't want
to go, but you're cross not to be asked.
Jilly Cooper

Why, a four-year-old child could understand this
contract. Run out and find me a four-year-old child. I
can't make head nor tail out of it.
Groucho Marx

I detest life insurance agents. They argue that I shall
one day die, which is not so.
Stephen Leacock

Without doubt, machinery has greatly increased the
number of well-to-do idlers.
Karl Marx

My father taught me to work. He didn't teach me to love it. **Abraham Lincoln**

By working faithfully for 8 hours a day you may eventually get to be a boss and work 12 hours a day. **Robert Frost**

Winning isn't everything, but wanting to win is. **Arnold Palmer**

If there are many applicants for a few jobs, the job is overpaid. **Milton Friedman**

Work expands so as to fill the time available for its completion. **Cyril Parkinson**

The only place where success comes before work is in a dictionary. **Vidal Sassoon**

One of the symptoms of approaching nervous breakdown is the belief that one's work is terribly important. If I were a medical man I would prescribe a holiday to every patient who believed their work to be important. **Bertrand Russell**

When business is bad, always start weeding out at the top. **Sir Graham Day**

People are like dogs. If you can't pay more, praise more. **Bjorn Wahlstrom**

The worst mistake a boss can make is not to say 'Well done'. **John Ashcroft**

Few great men could pass Personnel.   *Paul Goodman*

A diplomat is a person who can tell you to go to hell
in such a way that you actually look forward to the trip.
                                              Caskie Stinnett